JAZZY
Greeting Cards

JAZZY
Greeting Cards

Mickey Baskett

Sterling Publishing Co., Inc.
New York

PROLIFIC IMPRESSIONS PRODUCTION STAFF:

Editor in Chief: Mickey Baskett
Copy Editor: Phyllis Mueller
Graphics: Dianne Miller, Karen Turpin
Styling: Lenos Key
Photography: Jerry Mucklow
Administration: Jim Baskett

Library of Congress Cataloging-in-Publication Data
Baskett, Mickey.
  Jazzy greeting card / Mickey Baskett.
      p. cm.
  Includes index.
  ISBN 1-4027-2440-3
1. Greeting cards. I. Title.
TT872.B384 2005
745. 594'1--dc22

                                                    2005010573

10 9 8 7 6 5 4 3
Published in paperback in 2006 by Sterling Publishing Co., Inc.
387 Park Avenue South, New York, N.Y. 10016
©2005 Prolific Impressions, Inc.
Produced by Prolific Impressions, Inc.
160 South Candler St., Decatur, GA 30030
Distributed in Canada by Sterling Publishing
c/o Canadian Manda Group, 165 Dufferin Street
Toronto, Ontario, Canada M6K 3H6
Distributed in the United Kingdom by GMC Distribution Services,
Castle Place, 166 High Street, Lewes, East Sussex, England BN7 1XU
Distributed in Australia by Capricorn Link (Australia) Pty. Ltd.
P.O. Box 704, Windsor, NSW 2756 Australia
Printed in China
All rights reserved

Sterling ISBN-13: 978-1-4027-2440-4 Hardcover
        ISBN-10: 1-4027-2440-3
            ISBN-13: 978-1-4027-4055-8 Paperback
            ISBN-10: 1-4027-4055-7

For information about custom editions, special sales, premium and corporate purchases, please contact Sterling Special Sales Department at 800-805-5489 or specialsales@sterlingpub.com.

Contents

It's All in the Cards

 We seem to have run out of time. No time to write letters, no time to visit with friends on Sunday afternoon, no time to gather as a family for a meal together. We don't even have time to go shopping for a greeting card - we can just take a couple of seconds and email one. Let's take it DOWN a notch.

There isn't a more precious gift that you could offer to your friends or loved ones than taking the time to create a handmade, personal card. You are not only giving of your time, but you are giving of your creativity.

In creating this special card, you may find that you are not only giving, but you will also be getting. You will be getting a few minutes of stress-free relaxation as you cut, paste, stamp, stencil. You will be getting a special kind of joy that comes with creating art. You will be getting time to think about your friend or loved one as you create a special card.

So how do you go about creating a special card? This book will show you 60 great ideas for making handmade greetings. Stamping, collage, decoupage, pen and ink, colored pencil art, and stenciling are just a few of the techniques that are included here to start you on the road to creativity. The supplies section will familiarize you with the tools and materials you will need. Most craft stores, stamping shops, or shops specializing in scrapbooking will have everything you need. The projects include detailed, step-by-step instructions, as well as patterns when needed. Get started on a truly addictive craft. I know you can't make just one.

There isn't a more precious gift that you could offer
to your friends or loved ones than taking the time
to create a handmade, personal card.

PAPERS

Papers are the foundation of cards, and there is an infinite selection. As long as you can cut or tear and fold it, any paper can be used to make a card. How you plan to decorate the paper is the main consideration for selecting a particular paper. Papers also can be used to decorate cards and envelopes and make envelopes. When you mix and match different papers and paper elements, the possibilities are endless.

■ Purchased Blank Cards

The most convenient way to make a card is to start with a purchased card - a pre-cut blank that usually comes with an envelope. Card blanks come in a huge array of sizes, shapes, colors, textures, and finishes. You can purchase card blanks and envelopes at crafts stores, rubber stamp shops, and stores that sell art supplies, stationery, and office supplies.

■ Card Stock

Print and copy shops have a vast selection of card stock papers that are reasonably priced. Many papers offered by professional printers include matching envelopes. If not, consider purchasing coordinating papers in text (not card) weights to make your envelopes.

A print shop is an excellent source for large sheets of paper, ideal for making accordion-fold or oversized cards. For cards with several layers, consider lighter-weight papers. Most papers carried by print and copy shops are suitable for printing with a laser printer or copier, in addition to stamping and other methods of decorating and lettering. Other sources for papers are art supply stores, rubber stamp shops, and crafts stores.

■ Handmade Paper

Handmade papers can be used for an entire card or for embellishing. Many contain dried botanicals or other interesting elements. Some are beautifully marbled or silk-screened with a design. They may be more porous or thicker - but not necessarily heavier - than standard card stock. Handmade papers are not recommended for use with laser-printers and copying machines. Try tearing (rather than cutting) the edges of handmade papers to give your card an elegant look.

Handmade papers are available at art, crafts, and stamp shops or by mail order. They may be offered in stationery-size or wrapping-paper size sheets.

Vellum

Vellums are translucent papers. The most common type is uncolored. You can also find them offered as card blanks with envelopes. Vellums are versatile and elegant; they should be a basic component of your card-making supplies. Vellums are available in a rainbow of colors, in many printed designs, and embossed.

Vellums can be printed by most laser printers and copiers and stamped or marked with dye-based inks. Vellum accepts acrylic paint very well. Stamping with pigment ink works if you heat-emboss (otherwise the ink never seems to dry, only to smear.)

Adhesives show through vellum, so if you can't hide your glue with stickers or appliques, punch small decorative shapes from double-sided adhesive to attach vellum at the corners.

Use vellums for wonderful envelopes that showcase your handmade card creations. It's widely available at crafts and stamp shops.

Embossed Paper

Embossed papers are an easy way to add texture. Many colors and embossed designs are available at craft and stamp stores. Don't forget embossed handmade papers and wallpapers for special effects.

Printed Paper & Wrapping Paper

A huge variety of decorative papers are readily available. Printed sheets and decoupage papers can be found at crafts and stamping stores. Use the whole sheet or cut out motifs for embellishing.

Sources for decorative papers and wrapping paper include card shops, grocery stores, paper outlets, and gift shops.

Watercolor Paper

Use this heavy-weight paper to make handpainted cards. Find it at art supply and crafts shops.

Photocopies

You can create your own colored paper with photos, cut-out images, or other flat objects, such as flowers and leaves, by photocopying them on a color copier. It's a good idea to arrange the images on an 8-1/2" x 11" or 11" x 17" sheet of paper and secure them in place before taking them to a copy shop. Keep in mind that most copiers can reduce and enlarge.

Decorative Specialty Papers

Specialty papers and materials are generally used for decoration and embellishment rather than an entire card. You'll find lots of paper materials for cards in the scrapbooking section of your crafts or department store. Here are some suggestions:

- Construction paper – a common school supply – is great for cutting out designs to use on the cards.
- Corrugated papers and waffle papers, for instant texture. They are available in a rainbow of colors and a variety of ridge widths and patterns.
- Decoupage papers, including revivals of lovely vintage prints.
- Tissue paper, in colors, prints, and pearlized finishes. Use double-sided tape or spray adhesives (not wet glue) with tissues for best results.
- Laser and die-cut designs created for scrapbooking, for framing other elements.
- Paper doilies and foil trims, for elegance and a feminine touch.
- Paper napkins, with their array of images and colors, can be used like other paper motifs - just separate the layers and use only the top printed layer. Treat the printed layer like tissue and use appropriate adhesives to glue the layer to a piece of white paper or vellum.
- Clip art from books, magazines, or the Internet, can be copied (and enlarged or reduced) on white or colored paper. Add color with markers, paint, or colored pencils.
- Metallic and hologram foils and films, for shimmer and sparkle. Many are adhesive-backed; they're also available on rolls. Kids love them.
- Two-tone papers are a different color on each side. Two-tone papers may be card stock or paper weight.
- Velveteen or suede papers add a beautiful look and feel. They can be stamped, although the design will look somewhat muted.
- Ephemera is a term for printed matter of passing interest. This can refer to things such as old letters, postcards, ticket stubs, newspaper clippings. Ephemera pieces are great for decorating your cards.

CUTTING & MEASURING TOOLS

A visit to the scrapbooking section of a craft store will reveal many options for cutting and measuring. Start with a few basics, then add others.

■ Craft Knife

The one tool (besides scissors) you must have is a craft knife. A sharp blade is essential - it will cut through card stock or paper with a single stroke and slight pressure. If you find yourself exerting excess pressure or having to re-cut, the blade is dull. Replace it!

■ Scissors

A good, **standard-sized scissors** will be your most-used tool. **Small scissors with very sharp points** are indispensable for cutting out small shapes for collage or applique.

Decorative edge scissors or paper edgers are wonderful for adding interesting and elegant edges. The types include pinking, scalloping, and deckle, among others.

■ Paper Cutters

Paper cutters or paper trimmers, with a sliding or swing-action blade, save lots of time when cutting basic squares and rectangles. Some types have interchangeable rotary blades for creating decorative edges.

■ Corner Cutters and Corner Punches

Corner cutters allow you to make professional-looking rounded or decorative corners on your card and card components.

■ Ruler

A metal or metal-edge ruler, at least 12" long (18" is better), is necessary for cutting straight edges with your craft knife. Don't use an inexpensive plastic ruler - the knife will damage it.

A thick, see-through **quilter's ruler** is wonderful for cutting and measuring, but it's a bit more costly. If your budget allows, get a ruler at least 12" long made of 1/4" thick clear acrylic with a right-angle grid - it's ideal for cutting and measuring.

■ Decorative Punches

You can achieve many different looks very quickly with punches, and they're fun to use. Some punch a small shape, usually 1/4" or less. (Be sure to save the punched-out shapes - they make great embellishments.) Larger punches come in a myriad of shapes and designs.

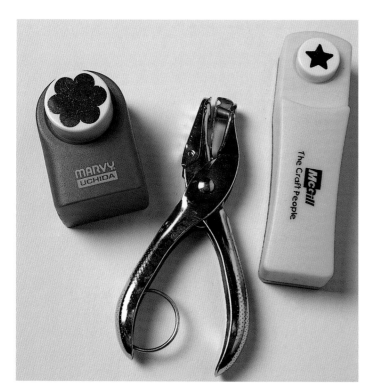

It takes practice to gauge exactly where the punch will occur, so practice on scrap paper before punching your card. Some punches have a longer "reach" so you can punch farther in from the edge of the paper; others allow you to only punch 1/4" or so from the edge.

■ Rotary Cutters

These tools make long, continuous cuts when used with a metal ruler or quilter's straight edge. Interchangeable blades make it possible to cut perforated lines and wavy and other decorative edges, but it's best not to use a straight edge with decorative blades.

■ Circle & Oval Cutters

Circle cutters make it possible to cut professional-looking circles. The cutter's adjustable arm can cut (or draw) perfect circles in any size you wish, from 1" to 8" in diameter. A similar tool allows you to draw or cut perfect ovals.

■ Cutting Mat

A self-healing cutting mat protects your work surface and helps extend the life of your blades. Most mats have a measuring grid - a most useful bonus. If you don't have a cutting mat, protect your work surface with heavy chipboard or matte board. Change it often - old cuts can make the knife blade veer off course and ruin a smooth slice.

■ Bone Folder

Bone folders are made of bone and are used to score paper for folding and to press sharp creases. An 8" size is best. Find bone folders at craft and art supply stores.

PAINTS & OTHER COLORING MEDIUMS

◼ Paper Paints

Paper paints are designed to work on just about any paper. You can add wonderful color, dimension, and accents to cards with paper paints. They are available in most craft shops.

Dimensional paper paints come in squeeze bottles with applicator tips, so they're easy to use for embellishing and writing. They can be used to create dimensional, textured, or flat finishes. You can thin this paint with a clear medium made specifically for it and use it for brush painting or use more medium and use the thinned paint like a wash.

The paper paints are acid free and, when dry, won't stick to other paper surfaces. They are flexible and won't crack as the paper bends, making them perfect for cards that will be mailed, and they don't distort the paper like many paints do.

◼ Acrylic Craft Paints

Acrylic craft paints, generally sold in 2 oz. bottles at crafts stores, are ideal for painted cards. Be aware, however, that the moisture in the paint may cause ripples, buckles, or other distortions to paper. (When the paint dries, the distortion may subside.) Always test acrylic paints on the paper you are using to be sure you will like the results.

◼ Watercolor Paints

Watercolor paints are useful for tinting and achieving a painterly effect. Like acrylics, they may affect some papers adversely, so test first.

◼ Paint Pens

Another way to add paint to cards is with **paint pens**, which are also called **metallic "leafing pens"**. They have a marker-type nib and are filled with lustrous paint in gold, silver, or copper. The ink dries quickly and is super for gilding the edges of cards and envelope flaps.

◼ Colored Pencils

Colored pencils are ideal for use with stamped images and stencils and to enhance painted areas. **Artist-quality colored pencils** are sold in craft and art supply stores individually and in sets. They are easy to use and the color transfers cleanly and smoothly. You control the intensity by applying light or heavy pressure, and shading and blending is easy.

Watercolor pencils are used for coloring, then brushed with water for painted effects.

◼ Applicators

Artist brushes are needed for painted designs and for working with watercolor pencils. Project instructions list the specific brushes you'll need.

Stencil brushes are short-handled brushes especially designed for stenciling. They come in a variety of sizes - the size you use depends on the size of the stencil openings (e.g., small openings require small brushes). Sponge brushes, foam sponges, and sponge-on-a-stick applicators also can be used for stenciling.

Use an old **toothbrush** with diluted paint for spattering (flyspecking).

Sponges such as natural sea sponges, cellulose sponges, sponge brushes, and sponge daubers can be used to apply paints.

◼ Markers

Air-erase pens are great for tracing marks and lines on paper - the marks fade away in 24 to 48 hours. Be sure to purchase an air-erase, *not* a water-erase pen when working on paper. Find them in fabric or scrapbooking departments of crafts stores.

Try **colored felt-tip pens**, **calligraphy pens**, **gel pens**, and **paint markers** for decorative treatments and writing. There are also markers made for inking stamps. The array of sizes and colors available is amazing. Find them at crafts, art supply, and office supply stores.

HEAT TRANSFER SUPPLIES

There are a number of products available that will allow you to transfer images and patterns that have been reproduced in color or black and white to paper and other soft materials. Images generated from magazines, newspaper, photo copies of photographs or art, and prints from inkjet and laser printers can be used.

■ Heat Transfer Tool

There are a variety of these tools on the market. Follow the manufacturer's instructions for using. In most cases, you lay the printed image face-down on your paper and rub the back of the image with the heat tool. Like magic the image is transferred to your paper. This is great to use for transferring wording on your greeting cards. Create a sentiment on your computer, then print. Be sure to reverse the letters when printing or when your transfer, your words will be a mirror image.

■ Heat Transfer Paper

There are many types of heat transfer paper available. Some are made especially to use with your computer. The images you print on them can be ironed onto your surface with a home iron. There are also transfer papers that can be used with a copier. Most scrapbooking or craft shops can help you find what is right for your purpose.

RUBBER STAMPS & INKS

Stamped images can be applied to paper with ink, markers, paint, and embossing powders. Rubber stamps can turn you into an artist - the only limitation is your imagination. If you have a sense of color and design, there's no stopping you. Here are some pointers.

There are different types of stamps. Some are full designs. Some have sentiments or greetings. There are small stamps and large stamps. There are outline stamps and background stamps. The raised areas of a stamp hold the ink and make the design, and the recessed areas remain colorless. Learn to look at your stamps as parts, and think of creating pictures and scenes with portions of your stamps by inking only the part of the stamp you want to use.

There are factory mounted stamps and unmounted rubber. Each stamp has a purpose, and no one kind is always best. Most stamps come as wood mounts - they are more expensive and probably of higher quality, but there are also stamps made of heavy foam rubber that will do the job for a fraction of the price. You can purchase the rubber and the wood and make your own stamps; another option is to have many unmounted rubber stamps and a few acrylic blocks to use instead of wood mounts.

Choosing Ink

The first ink choice you make is color. If you find the same color in different inks you have other choices to make - dye ink or pigment ink, large or small pad, raised or flat pad, rainbow or single color, metallic, fabric, waterproof, washable, tattoo, crafter's, petal points, embossing, memory ink - the list goes on. Some choices cost more. You need more than one ink pad, but you may not need them all.

The most significant difference in pads is the *type of ink*. All pads are either dye or pigment. Dye ink pads contain ink that is absorbed by the paper and dries fairly quickly. Pigment ink pads contain an ink that is thicker, stays on top of the paper, and takes longer to dry. The longer drying time makes pigment ink ideal for heat embossing, but if you stamp pigment ink on shiny paper or vellum, it will never dry.

Another difference is the *pad surface*. Stamp pads that are made of compressed fabric set in a frame can be re-inked when the pad becomes dry. They are available in many colors and aren't too expensive, but over time the middle of the pad breaks down and begins to sink, making it difficult to evenly ink a stamp. Also, you can only ink a stamp that is smaller than the frame. To address this, the industry created a raised surface of heavy felt or sponge. Neither breaks down in the middle, and you can easily ink a larger stamp on the raised pad. Raised surface pads are available in dye and pigment inks. Both are re-inkable, but you may find it easier and more economical to get a new pad.

Pads come in different sizes and shapes - traditional rectangles, squares, tiny squares, cat's eyes, huge, tiny, and so on. Some have lids that flip back. Little pads give you the option to have many colors at a lower price stored in a smaller space. You can ink a large stamp with a small pad if you turn your stamp (rubber up) and pat the pad over it.

In the **dye ink** family there are options. All dye inks are somewhat interchangeable unless you want a particular feature. Kids' pads and tattoo inks are both washable. Fabric ink is permanent; once heat set, it will not wash out. Memory ink is longer lasting, fades less, and is acid free. Waterproof ink won't run when used with watercolors or wet markers. There is even scented ink.

There are also options in the **pigment ink** family. Metallic colors add excitement. Watermark colors give an excellent first layer for further stamping. There are dozens of colors available. Embossing ink is pigment ink that has no color or a slight tint (but any pigment ink will work for embossing). Embossing ink's main advantage over colored ink is that it is easier to clean off your stamps and it has a slightly longer drying time.

Rainbow pads are available in dye and pigment inks. The colors in a dye ink rainbow pad usually are separated by spacers that you remove when you use the pad - once the barriers are removed, the colors run together. Eventually, you have a pad that does not have clear color separation - not a great investment. The best choice has a little lever that lets you slide the colors together when you want to use the pad and slide them apart before you put it away.

Because the ink is thicker, pigment rainbow pads do not run together - they hold their crisp color edges. There are several three- and five-color rainbow pads and a round pigment pad with eight different, removable triangles of color.

Another great way to ink a stamp is with **markers**. Any water-based marker can substitute for a dye ink pad. The markers made for stamping are best because their tips are intended to cover the surface efficiently. Using markers directly on a stamp allows you to produce a multi-colored image, and markers are ideal for traveling stampers.

Caring for Stamps

Be sure to clean your stamps after using them and especially before you ink a stamp with a new color. Use water, soap, baby wipes, or stamp cleaner, but don't use products that contain alcohol - it will dry out the rubber. An old washcloth and a soft toothbrush are good cleaning tools.

If you ink a stamp that is already loaded with another color, wipe the surface of the pad with a paper towel. The impression of the other color may be visible, but the excess ink will be gone.

Store your stamps and pads away from sunlight. Try the shallow plastic drawers that are available at discount stores or pizza boxes. Do not store ink pads in the refrigerator - they will dry out. Store the pads upside down to keep the ink in the top of the stamping surface.

Ink Applicators

A **brayer** is a useful tool for applying ink from a stamp pad to paper to create a colored background. *Interchangeable rollers* will allow you to create large areas of overall patterns.

Another handy ink applicator is the **dauber**. Daubers are small sponges, similar to tiny stamp pads, mounted on pen-size barrels. Many have a different color on each end. They are especially handy for use with small stamps and stenciled areas.

You can use **round sponge-tip applicators** (also called **stencil daubers**) to apply ink as well. These small domed sponges are attached to the end of a small dowel and can be used to transfer ink from a stamp pad to paper. Simply tap the sponge end against the stamp pad to load, then tap over a stencil opening to transfer the ink to the paper.

HEAT EMBOSSING SUPPLIES & TOOLS

Embossing is a dramatic stamping technique - the raised, shiny image gives a professional look to your art. It is easy to do once you understand how it works and what supplies to use.

First, you must use **pigment ink** to stamp your image. (Embossing ink is pigment ink that has no color or just a slight tint. It has a slightly longer drying time and is easy to clean off stamps.) Make sure your pad has a good amount of ink on it.

Second, you sprinkle the stamped image with **embossing powder** and it sticks to the wet ink. Embossing powder is made of little bits of plastic, and the size of the bits determines the type of embossing powder. "Detail" embossing powder, which has fine granules, is for use with stamps with fine lines and detail. "Extreme" embossing powders have larger granules for thicker images and sealing wax effects. Unless indicated, most embossing powders are all purpose with medium-size granules.

Third, you **heat** the powder and the powder melts, creating the image. You will get the best results with a heat gun or heat tool. They produce a very hot temperature with very little air flow. Some heat guns look like hair dryers, but don't be confused - a hair dryer would displace the powder and not get hot enough. (Heat guns are also used for shrink wrap and paint stripping.)

Here's How to Emboss

1. Stamp the image with pigment ink.
2. Sprinkle the image with embossing powder.
3. Hold the heat gun above the work and heat the image until all the powder has melted. You can see the color and texture change as it heats. Move the card around slightly to reach the entire image until it is all shiny. (The image will be dry and hot - much like melted wax.) Let cool, and don't touch it until it cools.

EMBOSSING TIPS

• **Work relatively quickly.** Take your time to get the image inked up and placed where you want it, then move right to the next step.
• **You can re-use excess powder.** Always place a sheet of folded paper under your work when you sprinkle the embossing powder. Shake the excess powder off the image and on the paper, then use the paper to pour the excess powder back in the bottle.

• **Colored or clear powder?** The color of the image is determined by the color of the embossing powder, unless you use clear powder - then the ink color determines the color of the embossed image.
• **Custom colors.** Embossing powders can be mixed. (You can find "recipe" books to help you get just the colors you want.) Experiment with small amounts of powders for the desired results.
• **Removing clinging powder.** If, after you pour the powder, you notice powder where you don't want it, brush it away with a soft paint brush or make-up brush. When working on black paper, the powder may stick to the paper and create a snowy effect. To avoid this, use a product you can rub on the paper to reduce the static cling so unwanted powder doesn't stick.
• **Try not to overheat** the powder - if you do, the image will flop, flatten, and burn.

Other Embossing Effects

Embossing pens are available in many colors and tip types, and the ink from just about any ballpoint pen can be used for embossing. (For best results, use an erasable ballpoint pen.) Just write your message, cover with powder, and heat. This is a very impressive way to sign your name.

For the look of **sealing wax**, use pigment ink for the base and sprinkle generously with a heavy embossing powder. Heat until it begins to melt and add more powder while it is hot. Keep melting and adding powder until you have a melted blob.

Stamp the hot blob with an inked stamp. Hold the stamp in place until the blob cools, then lift the stamp. You can cut around the impression with a punch or scissors.

To make an **embossed border**, take a two-way glue stick and run it down the edges of the card. Sprinkle with embossing powder and heat. You also can use heat-resistant double-face tape to hold the powder. Find the tape at stamping stores.

STENCILS

Stenciling is a technique for transferring designs to paper. Acrylic paints, stencil creams or gels, ink from a stamp pad, or colored pencils can be used to apply color through the openings of the stencil. Stencils also can be used to emboss designs.

Types of Stencils

Pre-cut stencils in a huge array of motifs and sizes are available at crafts stores. Stencils for use with paint and ink are generally made of **flexible, transparent plastic**; **metal stencils** are made specifically for embossing, but just about any stencil can be used to create embossed effects. Test your paper with your stencil to check for compatibility.

Applicators for Stencils

When applying paint, stencil creams or gels, or ink from a stamp pad, choose an applicator that corresponds with the size of the openings of the stencil. To apply larger stenciled images, consider using a stencil roller or a small painter's touch-up roller. You can also use sponge brushes, sponges, and sponge-on-a-stick applicators, which are available in a variety of sizes.

Embossing Tool

The best tool to use for embossing is a stylus with two different end sizes, but just about any stylus with round ball ends can be used for embossing.

Embossing with Stencils

To create a raised effect with a stencil, you work from the back of the paper with the stencil upside down and the paper on top of the stencil. Use the embossing tool to trace around edge of stencil. The thicker the stencil material, the deeper (more raised when turned right side up) the embossing will be.

Continued on next page

Stencil embossing a transparent paper, using a ball-end embossing tool or stylus.

Stenciling with acrylic paint, using a brush.

Outlining a stencil design with a colored pencil.

Stenciling with Paint & Ink

Stenciling is a dry-brush technique - you need very little paint or ink on the brush or other applicator. Dab or swirl the color on the paper through the openings in the stencil. Reload the brush as often as necessary to complete the design.

Stenciling with Colored Pencils

Colored pencils won't smear or seep, and they're great for outlining. With pencils, it's also easy to fill in the bridges (the gaps created by the stencil configuration) if you don't want the finished design to look stenciled.

ADHESIVES

You'll need a few different kinds of adhesives - there's not one universal glue for everything. What's best depends on the materials you're using.

■ Double-sided, Dry Adhesives

These are quick and accessible (double-stick tape is one). They may be too bulky for sheer papers, are best for small areas, and come in permanent and repositionable. Double-sided sheet adhesives, which have a paper liner on each side, can be cut to any size and shape - you peel away the liner from one side and apply it to one surface, then remove the second liner to attach the second surface. Save and use the small scraps.

Another type of dry adhesive comes in a dispenser and can be rolled on the back of the paper. It's permanent, so you can't undo a mistake. It's not at all bulky and doesn't show through sheer papers like tissue. (It does show through vellum, however.)

■ Glue Pens & Sticks

Liquid archival glue in a bottle with a small applicator tip (like a marker) is a good choice for small shapes and for sticking paper to paper. It dries fairly quickly, is permanent when dry, and is repositionable while wet. It isn't always strong enough for every kind of applique, and because it soaks in, it doesn't work well on porous surfaces. (Remember if it doesn't hold, you can always use a different adhesive.)

Glue sticks work with just about any kind of paper, dry fairly quickly, and are easy to apply.

■ Glue Dots

These are tiny dots of double-sided adhesive, available in a variety of tacks. They are not dimensional.

■ Jeweler's Glue

Use jeweler's glue for attaching unusual objects, such as charms, wire, or buttons. Get one that dries clear and sticks to all kinds of surfaces, particularly glass and metal. Use sparingly for best results.

■ Self-Adhesive Foam Dots

These are made of foam and have adhesive on both sides. They give **dimension** and adhere at the same time. Dimensional dots are generally used for adhering paper to paper, but they can secure lightweight objects. For less dimension, cut double-sided foam carpet tape to size. It's about half as thick as dimensional dots and can be stacked to any height you like.

■ Decoupage Medium

Decoupage medium can be used to glue and apply a protective topcoat to paper. Modern decoupage mediums are brush-on liquids that are clear-drying and non-toxic. You can find specialty decoupage finishes for antique, pearl, or sepia tones. There's also a decoupage finish that can be used with paint to create a crackled look.

■ Glitter Glue

Glue with glitter suspended in it comes in bottles or in pen-size containers - both with applicator tips so you can write or draw with it.

QUICK TRICKS WITH GLUE

Very personal cards can be made in an instant - all you need is paper, glue, and a decorative item. (This could be a photo, other ephemera, or a piece of memorabilia.

Here's how:

1. Cut one side of the paper with decorative scissors or tear with a deckle ruler. (This is the bottom of the card front.)
2. Measure the photo or other item you wish to glue to front of card. Add to the measurement the amount you wish to have as a margin around the item. (This is the size of the card front.)
3. Cut paper to allow for a front and a back. Fold in half.
4. Glue the item to front, using appropriate glue for the paper or the item you are gluing.

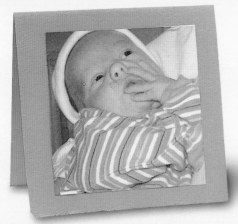

A special way to acknowledge times together is to glue a restaurant calling card or a ticket from a show you saw together.

Any card becomes special when you glue a photo on front. This is great for a baby announcement. You can also create a special birthday card by gluing a childhood photo of the person to whom you are sending the card.

Old postcards are great art - they are so very beautiful and nostalgic. Use a temporary adhesive to attach an old postcard to create a special bon voyage card.

Instant elegance. Use jewelry glue to glue a jewel to the front of a card. This makes a great thank you note or a gift card.

EMBELLISHMENTS

■ Beads & Jewels

Small beads (such as seed beads) and flat beads (such as leaves) can add dimension and interest to card designs. Attach them with jeweler's glue or dimensional paint - the applicator tip makes it easy to apply just a tiny dot. When the paint dries, it becomes part of the design.

You can also attach beads to cards with thread or wire, or make tassels and strands of beads on thread or wire to attach to cards.

Glue flat-backed beads, faceted jewels, and pieces of broken or outdated jewelry to cards with jeweler's glue.

■ Wire

Wire is available in many colors. Use it as a stand-alone decorative element or as a way to attach other decorations, such as buttons, beads, and charms. Lightweight wire (18 or 24 gauge) is best - you can bend it easily with your fingers. Cut it with round-nose pliers, wire cutters, or needlenose pliers.

■ Charms & Buttons

Charms and buttons on cards can be - well, charming. You'll find a huge selection of motifs at crafts and fabrics stores.

■ Ribbons, Cording, Threads & Yarns

Ribbons, cords, threads, fibers, and yarns can add texture, color, sparkle, and movement to cards. Since you need only small amounts for card decorating, this is a great way to use small scraps and pieces left from other projects. You'll see many examples in the projects sections

■ Stickers

Stickers are NOT just for kids anymore. There are great stickers available with charming designs for use with greeting cards. It's a quick way to decorate a card and matching envelope.

COLLAGE & LAYERING

Collage is an artistic composition of materials and objects on a surface. Many cards are collages - some very basic, some more complex. Layering is a type of collage that uses layers of paper for a decorative effect. All the layers are visible when the final layer is placed; most often the layers form borders or "frames" for the layer that follows.

A card collage might be layers of papers or start with papers and include charms, old postage stamps, buttons, wire, ticket stubs, or flattened bottle caps. Use adhesives that are appropriate for the elements in your collage - you may need to use different types at different stages of your composition.

Supplies for Collages

Any or all may be incorporated. There are no limits and no rules.
Papers for color and shape
Paper images (clip art, stamped images, photos, magazine clips, stickers, parts of other greeting cards)

Paper ephemera (ticket stubs, birth announcements, baseball cards, postage stamps or color photocopies of any of these)
Three-dimensional materials (dried botanicals, miniatures, ribbons, wire, beads, charms, buttons, feathers, stickers)
Adhesives

Basic Collage Method

1. Start with a card foundation. Lay out your materials and try different arrangements until you find one you like. It doesn't have to be exact at this point - you are just deciding what to include and what to save for another project.
2. Build your collage layer by layer, using adhesives appropriate to each connection. Avoid adding bulk, but ensure the adhesion between the layers is strong enough to hold as successive layers are added. If necessary, let each layer dry before proceeding to the next.

Basic Layering Method

1. Start with a card foundation. Try different combinations of papers until you arrive at an arrangement that pleases you.
2. Cut out the papers, making each successive layer smaller than the preceding one.
3. Glue the layers, using adhesives appropriate to each connection. Ensure the adhesion between the layers is strong enough to hold as successive layers are added. If necessary, set aside so each layer can dry before proceeding to the next.

WORKING WITH PHOTOS

It's nice to send photographs with cards, and even nicer to make the photo part of the card. Photocopies of your photographs or computer printouts of digital or scanned photos are not as bulky as photos, and they last longer. But if, for example, you are planning to send the same photo to many people at the same time (like a family photo at Christmas time or a birth announcement), the most economical and timesaving option may be to have the photo duplicated. Another option is to use a photo printer, if your photo is digital.

Photocopying Tips

- The best way to copy photos is on a color copier - even black and white photos look better when copied in color. Some copiers can copy your photos in a sepia tone, which gives them an old-time feel.
- If you have the time and the funds, copy the photos in a few different sizes. Most copiers use 8-1/2" x 11" or 8-1/2" x 14" paper; take advantage of the size and copy more than one photo on each sheet. When you start assembling your card, you will have lots of photos and sizes to pick from.
- Visit the copy store when it's not crowded. Many operators are glad to help if they don't have lots of customers waiting in line.

Frame Cards

The simplest way to show your photos is to attach them to a pre-made photo card that has a place for the photo and a built-in border. You can turn a simple photo into a framed picture just by giving it a photo card. There are different types of photo cards with choices in borders - embossed, decorative cut edges, edges with color, etc.

Look for a frame card that looks good with your photo.

Then decide what colors look good with your photo. It is easier to make a frame for a specific photo than to make a great frame and hunt down a photo to go in it.

Is there a design element in the photo that you can use on the frame? There are many ways to add your own touches.

- Use **rubber stamps** with small images and make a border with them. Or pick a large background stamp and create an all-over design. Or try a combination.
- Use **pens, markers, or dimensional paper paints** to make dots, swirls, and lines around the photo.
- Glue pieces of **decorative paper** or add **beads, buttons, or even puzzle pieces** around the frame.
- Use **pressed flowers, silk flowers, or appliques**.
- Use a **corner punch or corner cutter**. The simplest is a corner rounder. There are punches that give your corners many different looks and punches that you use on a separate paper that will make a decorative slot to slip your photo into.
- Trim the photo or cut the frame with **decorative edge scissors**.

But don't get so carried away that the photo gets lost. Sometimes simple is best.

Photo Collage

If just one picture won't do, a collage may be just the thing. Decide what pictures you want to use and arrange them, then cut away the parts you want to use. (TIP: Leave a little edge around the desired design to help pop it out.) Arrange them in a shape, fitting the pieces together like a puzzle, and mount on colored card stock. Or mount the pieces separately on colored paper. Enhance your photos with little bits of colored paper, glitter, buttons, beads, or memorabilia.

When you have a creation you like, photocopy it. That way, you can send it to more than one person.

Cards for
Special People
&
Special Times

Celebrate designated holidays like Mother's Day and
Father's Day and life passages like a graduation, a
wedding, a new home, or a new baby with a handmade
card. You can be sure the card you've sent will stand out
from the rest and be like no other the recipient will receive.
Acknowledge a one-of-a-kind friend with a one-of-a-kind
card. What's more special than that?

SUPPLIES

Paper:

Ivory blank card with deckle edge, 5" x 6-3/4"

Floral print paper

Polka dot paper

Adhesive-backed vellum

Clip art image - Butterflies

Tools & Other Supplies:

Rubber stamp - Floral

Ink pad - Red metallic

Walnut ink with small spray bottle

Paper adhesive

Computer and laser printer

Paper towels

Heat transfer tool

Iron

Scissors

Metal deckle edge ruler

INSTRUCTIONS

1. Mix walnut ink crystals with water according to manufacturer's instructions. Pour into a small spray bottle. Spray entire card with mixture. Pat dry with paper towel. Let dry. Iron card.

2. Stamp the front of the card, using the floral stamp with red metallic ink.

3. Using the deckle edge ruler, tear a 5" x 6" of floral paper and a 6" x 2-1/2" piece of polka dot paper. Crumple each piece of paper. Iron papers flat.

4. Apply adhesive to the back of each paper. Adhere polka dot paper to the front of the card, using the photo as a guide for placement. Adhere floral paper slightly to the top right of the polka dot paper.

5. Print clip art image on adhesive-backed vellum. Trim the image and apply to the front of the card, covering the two papers.

6. Type LOVE in the Papyrus font and print using a laser printer. Remember to reverse the image before printing.

7. Place the image face down on the top front of the card. Transfer the image using the hot transfer tool by rubbing the back of the image. ❑

SUPPLIES

Paper:

White card, 5" x 6-1/2"

Pink and blue plaid paper

White card stock

Pink card stock

Tools & Other Supplies:

Rubber stamp - "Special Delivery," stork, small baby motifs

Permanent stamping ink - Black

Colored pencils

3-1/2" yellow satin ribbon, 1/2" wide

14 blue eyelets

Self-adhesive dots

Scissors

Glue

Special Delivery

Birth Announcement Card

By Nancy Hamby

INSTRUCTIONS

1. Stamp all the designs on white card stock using black ink.

2. Color designs with pencils.

3. Cut a piece of plaid paper the size of the front of the card and glue in place on front of card.

4. Cut two strips of pink card stock 1-1/2" wide. Glue on the left and right edges of the card.

5. Cut out the small stamped motifs and glue to the pink strips as shown.

6. Cut out rectangles around the stamped stork and words. Glue each to a piece of pink card stock. Trim to make narrow borders.

7. Trim the ends of the ribbon in V-shapes and glue along the top.

8. Using adhesive dots, adhere the words on top of the ribbon.

9. Glue the stork at bottom center.

10. Embellish with eyelets as shown. ❑

With This Ring
Wedding Card

By Pat Schreiber

SUPPLIES

Paper:

Foam core board, 5" x 5"

White card stock, 10" x 5"

Tools & Other Supplies:

Lace, 8" x 8"

10" craft pearls on a string

2 decorative gold rings for embellishment

Tacky white glue

Glue stick

Spray adhesive

Ruler

Scissors

Craft knife

Pattern for Heart
(actual size)

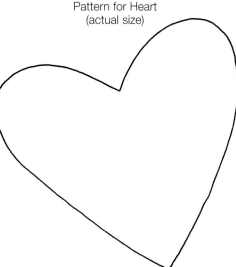

INSTRUCTIONS

1. Place the heart pattern in the center of the foam-core board. Using a craft knife and extreme caution, cut out the heart shape.

2. Cover the front of the foam-core board with adhesive from the glue stick and place in the center of the lace. Smooth lace over the board. Wrap the edges of the card and glue the excess lace to the back of the foam-core board. Make diagonal cuts radiating from the center of the heart. Fold back the lace to wrap the inner edges of the heart. Glue the excess to the back of foam board.

3. Fold the white card stock in half with the fold at the top of the card.

4. Place the heart pattern in the center of the front of the white card. Cut out the heart shape. (When the card is open, the back of the card will be solid and the front will have a cutout.)

5. Intersect the two gold rings and glue inside the card so they will show through the opening.

6. Glue the lace-covered foam board on the card front, using the glue stick.

7. Glue the pearls to the inside edge of the heart with white tacky glue. ❑

If Friends Were Flowers

Friendship Card

By Marni Adams

Card made from watercolor paper

Technical pens outline designs and borders

If friends were flowers, I'd pick you

Designs are colored with watercolor pencils then wet with brush for a painted look

Instructions begin on page 28.

sprinklz

SUPPLIES

Paper:

140 lb. soft press watercolor paper, 11" x 8-1/2"

Watercolor Pencils:

Black

Copenhagen

Crimson Red

Dark Green

Goldenrod

Mulberry

Blue

Olive Green

Spanish Orange

Ultramarine

Violet

Tools & Other Supplies:

Technical pens with black ink, .05, .08

Artist brushes - #2 round, #6 round

Tracing paper, graphite transfer paper, and stylus

Kneaded eraser

Pencil and sharpener

Ruler

Scissors *or* paper cutter

Paper towels

Water container

If Friends Were Flowers

Friendship Card

Pictured on page 27

INSTRUCTIONS

Prepare Card:

1. Fold watercolor paper to create vertical card 5-1/2" x 8-1/2".
2. Trace pattern and transfer design to front of card. Use a kneaded eraser to erase any mistakes.

Color:

1. With Goldenrod, color the backgrounds of the four corners and the backgrounds of the two horizontal bands in the center section. Use very light pressure.
2. With Crimson Red, color the background of the left section (using very light pressure), the flowers in the left section, and the side areas of the body of the ladybug.
3. With Violet, color the background of the right section (using very light pressure), the flowers in the right section, the top flower in the center section, the middle areas of the butterfly's wings, and every other circle in the dragonfly's body.
4. With Copenhagen, color the backgrounds of the top and bottom center sections (using very light pressure), the centers of the flowers in the top section, the flowers in the bottom section, and the center of the lower flower in the center section.
5. With Blue, color the background of the center section, using very light pressure.
6. With Dark Green, color the horizontal and vertical borders (using very light pressure) and half the leaves in the center section.
7. With Mulberry, color the upper areas of the butterfly's wings and every other circle in the dragonfly's body.
8. With Ultramarine, color the background areas of the butterfly's wings and the two letter "I"s in the message.
9. With Spanish Orange, color the dots on the lower part of the butterfly's wings and every other section of the bee's body.
10. With Olive Green, color half the leaves in the center bands.
11. With Black, color the butterfly's body, the ladybug's head and center body, and every other stripe on the bee's body.
12. Wet colored areas, using a brush dampened with water. Allow to dry overnight. TIPS: Every time you put the brush in water, blot on a paper towel. Use a #6 brush for larger areas, and a #2 brush for smaller areas.

Ink:

1. Using the .08 pen, ink the border lines and the dots.
2. Using the .05 pen, ink the remainder of the design. ❏

If friends were flowers, I'd pick you

©Sprinklz

SUPPLIES

Paper:

Green card stock,
  3-9/16" x 10-1/4"

White envelope, 3-5/8" x 6-3/8"

Tools & Other Supplies:

Daisy border punch

Garden stickers

Rubber stamp - "Plant Seeds of
  Friendship" and black dye ink
  pad *or* .03 black technical pen

Seed packet

Stylus

Ruler

Scissors

White tacky glue

Seeds of Friendship
Friendship Card

By Margaret Hanson-Maddox

Place seed packs
into pocket of card.

INSTRUCTIONS

Make & Decorate the Card:

1. Using the daisy border punch, punch design on each short end of the green card stock. Save the punched strips for the envelope.

2. Using the stylus, score the green card 3-1/2" from one punched border end.

3. Fold up the short flap on the larger section. Glue along the edges to form a pocket for the seed packet.

4. Stamp words or write them with a pen on the pocket.

5. Add stickers. Place seed packet in the pocket.

Decorate the Envelope:

1. Apply to each end of envelope the reserved strips from the punched border design.

2. Add a sticker. ❏

Card with matching envelope and seed pack in card pocket.

SUPPLIES

Paper:

White card, 6-1/2" x 5"

Blue checkerboard patterned paper, 4-1/4" square

Blue tile patterned paper, 3" square

Tools & Other Supplies:

Rubber stamp - Greeting ("The ornament of a house is the friends who frequent it")

Ink stamp pads - Cream, turquoise, black

Adhesive for paper

18" fiber (in colors to match patterned paper)

12" sheer green ribbon, 3/4" wide

Scissors

Wax paper

INSTRUCTIONS

1. Load stamp with cream ink and stamp randomly on card.

2. Color edge of card by sliding it along the edge of the turquoise stamp pad.

3. Cut swallowtails on each end of green ribbon. Glue to center of front and inside front of card.

4. Center tile patterned paper on checkerboard paper square and glue.

5. Load rubber stamp with black and stamp greeting in center of paper squares.

6. Lay the paper squares on wax paper. Run a bead of glue along outside edge. Attach fiber. Let dry.

7. Glue just above center of card. ❑

The Ornament of a House...
New Home Card

By Barbara Mansfield

The Music in My Life is You

Someone Special Card

By Pat Schreiber

SUPPLIES

Paper:

Foam-core board, 5" x 5"

Ivory cardstock, 10" x 5"

Rose mulberry paper, 8" x 8"

Tools & Other Supplies:

Rubber stamp of sheet music background design

Black dye-based inkpad

5 tiny silk roses to match mulberry paper

1-1/2 yds. of 1/8" wide pink ribbon

12" length of craft pearls

Tacky white glue

Glue stick

Ruler

Scissors

Craft knife

Pink marker (optional)

INSTRUCTIONS

1. Measure 1-1/2" from all sides of the foam-core board and mark a 2" square in the center of the foam-core board. Using a craft knife and extreme caution, cut out the 2" square.

2. Cover the front of the piece with glue from the glue stick and place in the center of the mulberry paper. Smooth paper in place. Wrap the paper around the edges of the card and glue the excess mulberry paper to the back of the card. Cut an "X" in the center square. Wrap the paper over the edges of the center square and glue the excess to the back of piece. If any white is showing in the corners, color with a pink marker or attach small pieces of mulberry paper.

3. Fold the 10" x 5" ivory cardstock in half placing the fold at the top of the card. This will be the base card.

4. Using the sheet music rubber stamp and black inkpad, stamp the design on the center front of the base card.

5. Glue the covered foam-core board onto the base card, making sure the sheet music designs shows through the opening.

6. Fold the length of pearls in half, forming a loop at the top. Place roses on top of loop. Fold ribbon into thirds and tie a bow around the pearls and roses. Using white tacky glue, glue the pearls and ribbons on the upper left corner of card. ❏

SUPPLIES

Paper:

Yellow gold card, 5" x 7"

Gold metallic paper

Yellow gold paper

Mulberry paper

Web paper

Tools & Other Supplies:

Rubber stamp - "For My Father," plus various small motifs, e.g., coins, knife, chess pieces, feathers, keys

Pigment inks - Gray, rust, brown, black, silver, gold

Cosmetic sponge

Embossing powder - Gold, silver, black

Heat gun

Assorted charms, clips, chains

4 copper corners

Copper paint pen

Craft knife and cutting mat

Glue

INSTRUCTIONS

This is a collage card, which means anything goes.

1. Stamp designs randomly on the card front, using different inks. Let dry.
2. Sponge lightly and randomly with inks. Let dry.
3. Glue a piece of mulberry paper and a piece of web paper on the card.
4. Cut a piece of yellow gold paper 3" x 3-1/4". Stamp randomly with motifs and allow to dry.
5. Stamp "For My Father" on the yellow panel with gold ink. Emboss with gold powder.
6. Edge yellow panel with copper ink and apply the copper corners. Mount on piece of gold metallic paper. Trim.

Father's Day Charms
Father's Day Card

By Nancy Hamby

7. Stamp the smooth charms with various motifs using black ink. Emboss stamped designs with black powder.
8. Edge the card with copper ink.
9. Arrange charms and chains and clips on front of card. Glue in place.
10. Glue "For My Father" panel on card and embellish with additional charms and clips. ❏

SUPPLIES

Paper:

Navy blue card stock,
   8-1/2" x 5-1/2"

Rust card stock, 4-1/4" x 5-1/2"

Cream card stock,
   8-1/2" x 5-1/2"

Tools & Other Supplies:

Rubber stamps - Map
   background, fishing quoteInk
   pad - Navy

Oval templates *or* oval cutters

Glue stick

INSTRUCTIONS

Fold & Stamp:

1. Fold the navy blue card stock in half with the fold on the left side to make a card 4-1/4" x 5-1/2".

2. Fold the cream card stock in half with the fold on the left side to make a card 4-1/4" x 5-1/2".

3. Stamp the front of the cream card, using the map background stamp with navy ink.

Cut Ovals:

Before each cut, check to make sure the ovals will align properly when card is assembled.

1. Cut a 2-1/2" x 3-1/4" oval in the center of the rust card stock.

2. Cut a 2-3/4" x 3-1/2" oval in the center of the front of the cream card stock.

3. Cut a 3" x 3-7/8" oval in the center of the front of the navy card stock.

Assemble:

1. Stamp the center of the inside of the cream card with a fishing quote.

2. Glue the rust card stock to the back of the inside front

Hook, Line & Sinker

Someone Special Card

By Pat Schreiber

of the cream card. TIP: Before gluing, check the alignment of the ovals.

3. Apply glue to the back *only* of the cream card. Place inside the navy card. (This arrangement puts the navy card outside and provides a double front cover.)

4. Trim the outside edges, if necessary. ❑

Invitation of Special Occasion Card

By Pat Schreiber

SUPPLIES

Paper:

White card stock, 8-1/2" x 5-1/2" and 6" x 5-1/2"

Magenta suede paper, 1-1/2" x 4-1/4"

Tools & Other Supplies:

7" magenta satin ribbon, 1/2" wide

3 black beads, 5mm

Paper crimper

Ruler

Glue stick

White tacky glue

INSTRUCTIONS

1. Fold the 8-1/2" x 5-1/2" white card stock in half, placing the fold on the left side of card.

2. Crimp 2" of the 6" x 5-1/2" white card stock. Release pressure and move the card stock forward 1/2" for the shirt center. Crimp 2" more.

3. Trim the crimped card to measure 4-1/4" x 5-1/2". Make sure the uncrimped section is in the vertical center. Using the glue stick, adhere to the white folded card.

4. Tie a small bow with the magenta ribbon. Glue in place with white glue at the top edge of the card in the center.

5. Measure 1" from the top edge of card. Glue a black bead with white tacky glue at the center of the smooth card. Measure down 1-1/8" and glue another bead. Measure 1-1/8" again and glue the last bead.

6. Glue the magenta suede paper across the bottom of the card. ❑

Congratulations, Graduate

Graduation Card

By Pat Schreiber

INSTRUCTIONS

1. Trace pattern from book onto tracing paper. Transfer pattern to marbled card stock and suede paper. Cut out.

2. Using a glue stick, glue the marbled card stock pieces to the backs of the suede paper pieces.

3. Cut a piece of marbled card stock 3-1/4" x 5-3/4". Fold in half to make a card with the fold at the top edge.

4. Stamp "Congratulations" inside the card with clear ink. Sprinkle with gold embossing powder and emboss with heat gun.

5. Position the bottom of the cap over the folded card. Glue in place.

6. Cut a circle from the suede paper. Stick on top of a foam dot. Color white edge of the foam dot with a burgundy marker. Allow to dry.

7. Adhere the complete foam dot in the center of the top of the cap.

8. Loop the tassel over the foam dot and glue in place.

9. Position the top of the cap over the card and mount with foam dots for a dimensional look. ❑

Pattern can be found on page 38

Pattern can be found on page 38

SUPPLIES

Paper:

1 sheet burgundy suede paper

1 sheet marbled burgundy card stock

Tools & Other Supplies:

Tracing paper, pencil, transfer paper, stylus

Rubber stamp - "Congratulations"

Gold embossing powder

Heat gun

Pigment ink pad - Clear

Self-adhesive dots

Burgundy marker

Scissors

Small cream Tassel

Glue stick

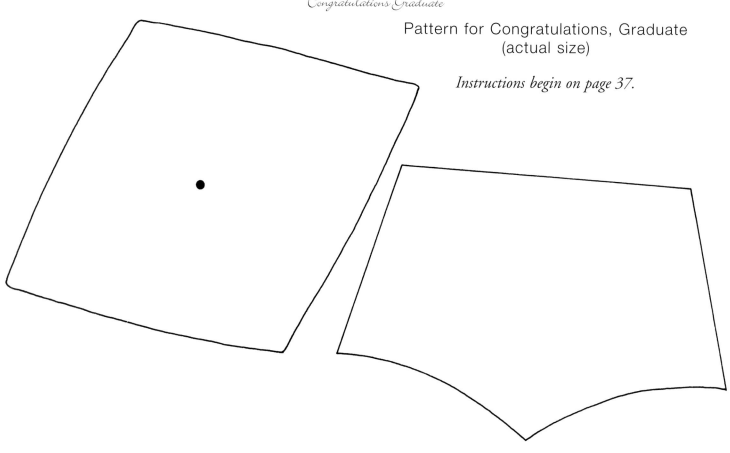

Pattern for Congratulations, Graduate
(actual size)

Instructions begin on page 37.

Pattern for Friends & Flowers
(actual size)

Instructions begin on page 42.

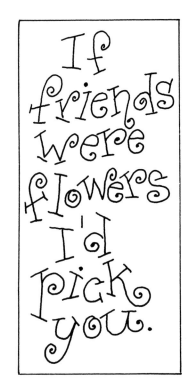

Pattern for Love You Beary Much (actual size)

Instructions begin on page 40.

Love You Beary Much
Someone Special Card

By Marni Adams

INSTRUCTIONS

Prepare the Card:

1. Fold watercolor paper to create a vertical card 5-1/2" x 8-1/2".

2. Trace the pattern. Using graphite paper, transfer design to front of card (except shading lines on bear's cheeks and ears and details on yellow border patches). Use a kneaded eraser to erase any mistakes.

Color with Watercolor Pencils:

1. With Canary Yellow, color the top center square, the fifth square from the top on the right, and the fifth square from the top on the left.

2. With Sunburst Yellow, color the top right corner square, the seventh square from the top on the right, the square on the bottom left, and the third square from the top on the left.

3. With Spanish Orange, color the third square from the top on the right, the square on the bottom right, the top left square, and the seventh square from the top on the left.

4. With Blush Pink, color the large heart in the center, the background of the pink square on the top left, the background of the fourth square from the top on the right, the background of the bottom right corner square, and the background of the sixth square from the top on the left.

5. With Pink, color "You," the background of the pink square on the top right, the background of the bottom center square, and the background of the fourth square from the top on the left.

6. With Orange, color the background of the second square from the top on the right, the background of the sixth square from the top on the right, background of the second square from the top on the left, and the background of the bottom left corner square.

7. With Poppy Red, color "Much," the heart in the second square from the top on the right, the center of heart in the fourth square from the top on the right, the heart in the second square from the top on the left, and the heart in the bottom left corner.

8. With Carmine Red, color "Love," the double hearts in the top right corner, the heart in the sixth square from the top on the right, the four hearts in the bottom center square, and the heart in the fourth square from the top on the left.

9. With Crimson Red, color "Beary," the border of the center heart, the inner border, the heart in the top left corner, the border of heart in the fourth square from the top on the right, the heart in bottom right corner, and the two hearts in the sixth square from the top on the left.

10. With Sienna Brown, color the bear's inner ears and muzzle.

11. With Dark Brown, color the bear.

12. With Black, color the bear's eyes and nose and the outer border.

13. With Violet Blue, color the background of the center using very light pressure.

14. Wet colored areas, using a brush dampened with water. TIPS: Every time you put the brush in water, blot on a paper towel. Rinse thoroughly between colors. Use the #6 brush for larger areas and the #2 brush for smaller areas. Allow to dry overnight.

Ink:

1. Using graphite paper, transfer the details of the yellow border patches. Use a kneaded eraser to erase any mistakes.

2. Using the .08 pen, ink the border lines, border of the center heart, and the dots.

3. Using the .05 pen, ink the hearts in the border.

4. Using the .03 pen, ink the remainder of the design.

Color with Colored Pencils:

1. With the Blush Pink pencil, color details of top center square.

2. With the Pink pencil, color details of third square from the top on the right and the seventh square from the top on the left.

3. With the Orange pencil, color details of the seventh square from the top on the right and the third square from the top on the left.

4. With the Carmine Red pencil, add shading to bear's ears and cheeks and color the details of the fifth square from the top on the right and the fifth square from the top on the left.

5. With the Poppy Red pencil, color details of the yellow squares on the bottom right and top left corner.

6. With the Crimson Red pencil, color details of top right corner square and the yellow square on the bottom left. ❏

SUPPLIES

Paper:

Card, 140 lb. watercolor paper, 5" x 6-7/8"

Envelope, 5-1/4" x 7-1/4"

140-lb. watercolor paper, 8-1/2" x 11"

Dotted lime green scrapbook paper, 4-5/8" x 6-1/2"

Pink card stock, 4-3/4" x 3"

White card stock, 3-7/8" x 1-3/4" and 5-1/4" x 3-1/4"

Paper Paints:

Amethyst (metallic)

Baby Pink

Blue Sapphire (metallic)

Calypso Sky

Dioxazine Purple

Engine Red

Fresh Foliage

Green Forest

Pumpkin Orange

School Bus Yellow

Wicker White

Flow medium (to thin the paint for stroke work)

Tools & Other Supplies:

Paint brushes - #5 round, 1/4" angled shader

Pink fine tip scrapbook marker

Tracing paper, trasnfer paper, stylus

Scissors

4 large self-adhesive dots

4 small self-adhesive dots

4" green/yellow ribbon, 3/8" wide

Glue stick

Double-sided tape adhesive

Friends & Flowers
Friendship Card

By Karen Embry

INSTRUCTIONS

Paint:

1. Trace pattern from book. Transfer the flower designs to watercolor paper.

2. Paint the round flower (rose) with Baby Pink. Float the bottom edge and inside the center of the flower with Engine Red.

3. Paint the wavy-edged flower with Calypso Sky. Float the edge and inside the center with a mix of Calypso Sky + Blue Sapphire.

4. Paint the four-petal rounded edge flower with a mix of Amethyst + Wicker White. Float the edge of the flower and inside the center with Dioxazine Purple.

5. Paint the five-petal flower with School Bus yellow. Float the edges of the petals and inside the center with Pumpkin Orange.

6. Paint the leaves on all of the flowers with Fresh Foliage. Float the edges with Green Forest. Let dry.

7. Paint one flower (mine is a rose) at the bottom of the envelope.

Assemble:

1. Cut out the flowers and leaves.

2. Center and glue the green dotted scrapbook paper in the center of the card.

3. Center the larger piece of white card stock on the green paper.

4. Glue the pink card stock in the center of the white card stock.

5. Transfer the saying to the smaller piece of card stock. Using the pink marker, write the words. *Option:* Letter the words freehand.

6. Glue the piece of white card stock with the words at the center of the pink card stock.

7. Place one large adhesive dot on the back of each flower and one small adhesive dot on the back of each leaf.

8. Adhere flowers to the card as shown in the photo.

9. Tie ribbon in a bow and glue at the center top of the card. ❑

Pattern can be found on page 38.

If friends were flowers I'd pick you.

Happy Birthday Cards

Make someone's birthday a true cause for celebration
with the gift of your time. Making your own birthday cards
allows you to customize the message and the
embellishments for the recipient and customize
for special birthdays.

Never Grow Old

Birthday Card

By Sandra Wild

INSTRUCTIONS

1. Fold black card stock in half to make card 8-1/2" x 5-1/2". Crease fold with a bone folder.

2. Cut gingham paper diagonally with deckle scissors to fit left side of card. Glue in place.

3. Stamp "Happy Birthday" in frost white at top of card.

4. Insert brads in holes of black circle tags. Glue to card front.

5. Mount domed numbers on tags.

6. Print favorite sentiments on computer. (I used the Invitation font and 24-pt. type.)

7. Trim one sentiment with deckle scissors to fit card. Glue in place.

8. Trim another sentiment with deckle scissors to 4" x 2-1/4". Glue to piece of checked paper 4-1/2" x 2-3/4". Glue inside card.

9. Loop ribbons around folded edge of card and tie.

10. Cut a piece of gingham paper to cover one corner of the envelope and glue in place. ❏

Celebrate with a Cupcake

Birthday Card

By Karen Embry

Designs painted with paper paint

Watercolor paper card

Rhinestones in assorted colors

Lettering with scrapbook markers

Instructions begin on page 48.

SUPPLIES

Paper:

Watercolor paper card,
    5" x 6-7/8"

Envelope, 5-1/4" x 7-1/4"

Paper Paints:

Baby Pink

Blue Sapphire (metallic)

Calypso Sky

Disco (glitter)

Engine Red

Fresh Foliage

Green Forest

Linen

Pumpkin Orange

Sahara Gold (metallic)

School Bus Yellow

Wicker White

Flow medium (to thin the paint)

Tools & Other Supplies:

Black permanent fine-tip
    scrapbook marker

16 round rhinestones, 1/8" -
    Assorted colors

Glue dots, 1/8"

Transfer paper, tracing paper,
    and stylus

Celebrate with a Cupcake
Birthday Card

Pictured on page 47

INSTRUCTIONS

Paint:

1. Transfer the design.

2. Paint the party hat and one streamer at the top of the hat with Calypso Sky. Float the bottom edge with Sapphire Blue. Paint the dots on the hat with Pumpkin Orange. Float the bottom edges of the dots with Engine Red.

3. Paint coordinating dots on the envelope.

4. Paint one streamer on the top of the hat with Baby Pink and float with Engine Red. Paint another streamer with School Bus Yellow and float with Pumpkin Orange. Paint another streamer with Pumpkin Orange and float with Engine Red. Paint another streamer with a mix of Baby Pink + Engine Red. Paint the remaining streamer with Fresh Foliage.

5. Paint the icing with Baby Pink and float the bottom edge with a mix of Engine Red + Baby Pink.

6. Paint the candle with Wicker White. Paint the lines on the candle with Baby Pink and Engine Red.

7. Paint the cupcake paper with Linen. Float the bottom with Sahara Gold. Paint the lines in the paper with Sahara Gold.

8. Paint the candle flame with School Bus Yellow. Float one side of the flame with Pumpkin Orange.

9. Paint the candy sprinkles on the icing, alternating colors. Let dry.

10. Brush a thin coat of glitter Disco on the icing and candle flame.

11. Paint the bow with Fresh Foliage. Float the left side with Green Forest. Paint the lines with School Bus Yellow.

Decorate:

1. Letter the words "Happy Happy Birthday" with the scrapbook marker.

2. Attach the rhinestones with glue dots randomly over the front of the card on the unpainted areas. ❏

Pattern for Card (actual size)

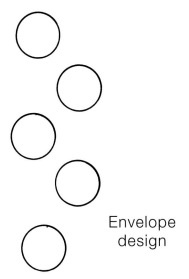

Envelope design

SUPPLIES

Paper:

White card, 5" x 6-1/2"

White card stock

Black card stock

Red paper with white dots

Black plaid paper

Tools & Other Supplies:

Rubber stamps - Picnic table with words, hot dog with ants, oven mitt, utensils, condiments

Colored pencils

Permanent stamping ink - Black

6" sheer black ribbon, 7/8" wide

Fine-tip black marker

Craft knife and cutting mat

Glue

INSTRUCTIONS

1. Stamp the hot dog stamp along the top and bottom of the card with black ink. Color with pencils.

2. Stamp the picnic table with words, oven mitt, utensils, and condiments on white card stock with black ink. Color with colored pencils.

3. Cut out a rectangle around the stamped picnic table and glue on dotted paper to make a border, then on black card stock.

4. Cut a piece of black plaid paper to fit between the lines of hot dogs. Glue the ribbon along the right side of the plaid paper, folding the ends of the ribbon over the paper and securing with glue. Glue plaid panel to front of card.

5. Cut a strip of dotted paper. Glue on top of the ribbon.

6. Glue the picnic table panel on the plaid panel as shown.

Life's a Picnic

Birthday Card

By Nancy Hamby

7. Cut out the remaining stamped pieces and glue over the ribbon.

8. Outline all the stamped panels with a black marker. ❏

Presents & Balloons

Birthday Card

By Nancy Hamby

SUPPLIES

Paper:

White card, 5" x 6-1/2"

Card stock - White, yellow, purple, pink

Tools & Other Supplies:

Rubber tamps - "Happy Birthday," birthday balloons, gifts, party hats, ice cream

Permanent stamping ink pad - Black

Pigment inks - Yellow, blue, green, purple, fuchsia

Colored pencils

Self-adhesive dimensional dots

Natural sponge

INSTRUCTIONS

1. Stamp the balloon stamp with black ink on the front of the card. Color with pencils.

2. Use a sponge to lightly sponge all the ink colors over the front of the card, the envelope flap, and a piece of white card stock where you will stamp the words. Stamp the words with black ink.

3. Cut out a rectangle with the words and glue to yellow, then pink, then purple card stock to make a border.

4. Stamp the packages, ice cream, birthday cake, and hats on white card stock. Color with pencils. Cut out, using scissors.

5. Reserving three cutouts for the envelope, glue the colored cutouts on the front of the card as shown, using adhesive dots to lift the hats and ice cream cones.

6. Line the edge of the card with a black marker.

7. Glue the three reserved cutouts to the envelope flap. ❏

Roses for Your Birthday

Birthday Card

By Pat Schreiber

INSTRUCTIONS

Fold & Decorate the Card:

1. To begin making this tri-fold card, fold the right side of the sage card stock to the left 3-1/2".

2. Using the deckle ruler or a random tearing pattern, tear off 1/2" of the left side of the paper. Fold the left side of the card to the right 3-1/4". (The folded card should measure 4-1/4" x 5-1/2".)

3. Cut a 2-5/8" x 5-1/2" strip of burgundy paper and glue to the front of the left fold 1/8" from the side fold.

4. Cut a 2-1/2" x 5-1/8" strip of script paper. Tear a deckle edge down both the left and the right edges. Center this strip over the burgundy strip and glue in place. Glue this section on the left front fold of the card, placing it 1/8" from the fold.

5. Cut a strip 3-1/4" x 5-1/2" of antique gold paper. Cut a strip 2-1/4" x 5-1/2" of script paper. Tear a deckle edge down the right edges of both pieces. Glue the antique gold paper near the right folded edge, using the photo as a guide. Glue the script paper on top of the gold paper, lining up the left edges.

Make the Greeting Piece:

1. Cut a sage green rectangle 3-1/4" x 2-3/4". Tear a deckle edge around the edges to a create piece 2-3/4" x 2-1/4".

2. Cut a burgundy rectangle 2-1/2" x 2". Center and glue on top of the green rectangle.

3. Cut a cream rectangle 2-1/4" x 1-3/4". Stamp "Happy Birthday" with burgundy ink in the center of the cream rectangle.

4. Center and glue the stamped rectangle on the burgundy rectangle.

5. Glue the greeting piece to the left folded side *only*, positioning it an angle.

6. Use white tacky glue to attach the rose to the lower left corner of the birthday greeting. ❑

Happy Birthday Dots

Birthday Card

By Pat Schreiber

SUPPLIES

Paper:

Red card stock, 5-1/2" x 8-1/2"

Yellow card stock, 5-1/4" x 4"

Navy blue card stock,
    5" x 3-3/4"

White card stock,
    4-1/2" x 3-1/4"

Tools & Other Supplies:

Round foam-tipped
    applicators, 1/2"

Paper paints - Red, Blue,
    Yellow, Green

12" *each* of blue, yellow,
    and green curling ribbon

24" red curling ribbon,
    cut in two 12" pieces

Glue stick

Scissors

Stapler

INSTRUCTIONS

1. Fold red card stock in half with the fold at the top to form a card 5-1/2" x 4-1/4".

2. Center and glue the blue card stock on the yellow card stock.

3. Using paper paints and round foam-tipped applicators, randomly press circles in all four colors on the white card stock. Allow to dry.

4. Using the writing nozzle on the Red paint bottle, write "Happy Birthday." Let dry.

5. Glue the painted white card at an angle on the blue card stock.

6. Using the edge of the scissors and great care, curl each piece of ribbon.

7. Align one end of each ribbon piece and staple together. Glue under the upper left edge of the yellow card. Center and glue the yellow card stock on the folded red card. ❑

SUPPLIES

Paper:

White card stock, 8-1/2" x 11"

Dark green decorative paper,
    8-1/2" x 11"

Tools & Other Supplies:

Rubber stamp with greeting of
    your choice

Purple ink pad

Gold glitter and adhesive

Grape paper appliques, 2

Metallic gold pen

Scissors

Glue stick

Rectangle template for cutting
    hole in card (optional)

INSTRUCTIONS

1. Cut a rectangle measuring 3-1/4" x
   4-1/2" from the white cardstock.

2. Stamp the white card with quote or
   greeting. Set aside to dry.

3. Fold the green paper in half lengthwise to measure 4-1/4" x 11".
   Transfer the wine bottle shape to
   the piece of green paper, placing
   the pattern on the fold. Cut out
   bottle shape.

4. Measure down 5-1/2" from the top
   of the bottle and cut a window
   2-1/4" x 3-1/2" from the front of
   the bottle. Use a rectangle template
   or cut using pattern given.

5. Edge the window with a gold
   metallic pen.

6. On the front of the green wine
   bottle shape, measure down from
   the top 3-1/4" and mark. Cover the
   top of the wine bottle down to this
   mark with glitter adhesive. Sprinkle
   gold glitter over adhesive.

A New Day

By Pat Schreiber

7. Glue the white card to the inside of the green wine bottle so that the greeting shows through the rectangle cut in green bottle shape.

8. Glue the wine bottle shapes together to provide body for the card. This card does not open.

9. Glue two grape clusters to the front of card as shown. (Alternative to purchased grapes is to use a regular hole punch and punch 12 holes in purple paper and light green paper. Assemble into a grape cluster raising the top layer with micro pop dots. Cut a tiny brown stem and glue to the back of the cluster. Attach to card.) ❑

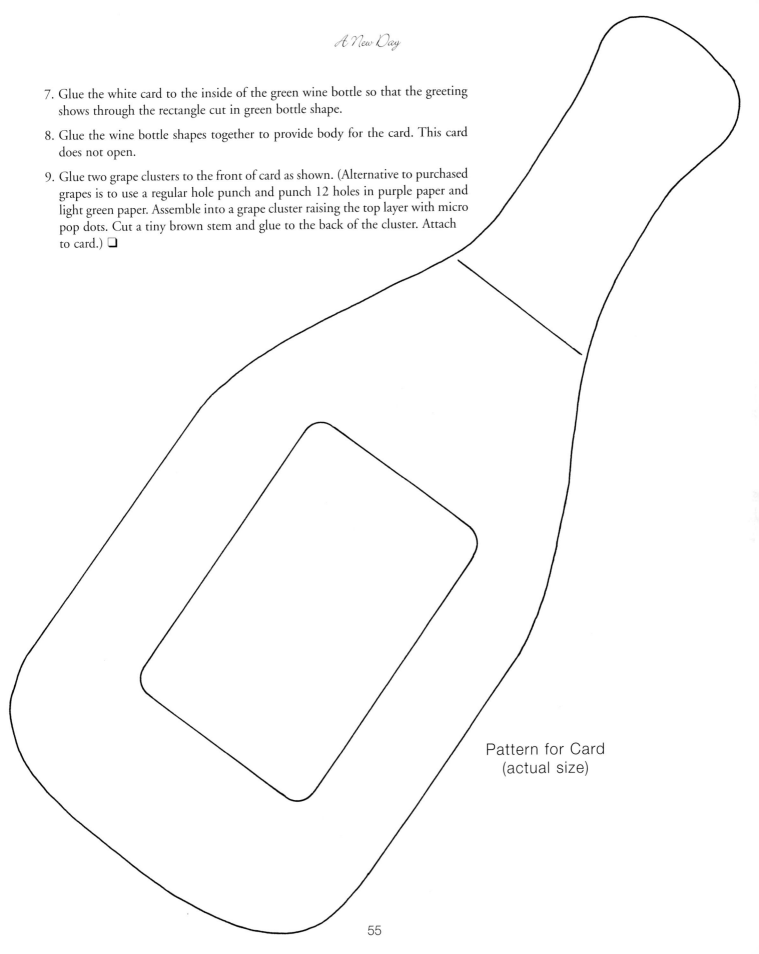

Pattern for Card
(actual size)

SUPPLIES

Paper:

140 lb. soft press watercolor paper, 5-1/2" x 8-1/2"

Acrylic Craft Paints:

All are metallic colors.

Amethyst

Aquamarine

Blue Sapphire

Emerald Green

Garnet Red

Inca Gold

Pearl White

Periwinkle

Plum

Glazing medium

Tools & Other Supplies:

Technical pens with black ink, .05, .08

Artist brushes - #2 round, #6 shader

Wet palette or foam plate

Kneaded eraser

Pencil and sharpener

Paper towels

Water container

Tracing paper, transfer paper, and stylus

Happy Happy Birthday
Birthday Card

By Marni Adams

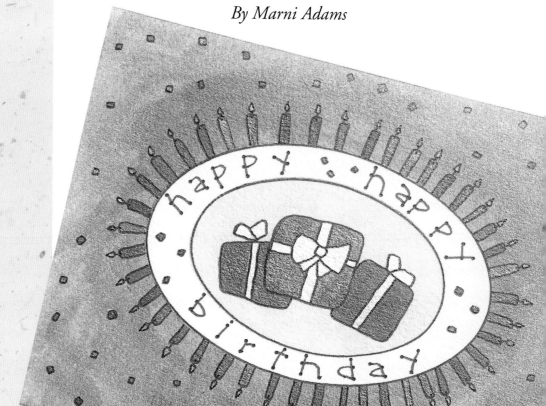

INSTRUCTIONS

Prepare Card:

1. Fold watercolor paper to create a horizontal card 5-1/2" x 4-1/4".

2. Trace pattern and transfer oval border lines *only*. Use a kneaded eraser to erase any mistakes.

Paint Using the #6 Shader:

1. Mix equal amounts glazing medium and Inca Gold. Paint center oval.

2. Mix equal amounts glazing medium and Pearl White. Paint outer oval.

3. Mix equal amounts glazing medium and Periwinkle. Paint the background. Let dry.

4. Using graphite paper, transfer the remainder of the design. Use a kneaded eraser to erase any mistakes.

Paint Using the #2 round brush:

1. With Pearl White, paint the ribbons on the packages.

2. With Inca Gold, paint the candle flames.

3. With Periwinkle, paint the middle package, seven candles, and eight pieces of confetti.

4. With Amethyst, paint the left package, six candles, and eight pieces of confetti.

5. With Emerald Green, paint the right package, six candles, and eight pieces of confetti.

6. With Aquamarine, paint six candles and eight pieces of confetti.

7. With Plum, paint six candles and eight pieces of confetti.

8. With Garnet Red, paint six candles and seven pieces of confetti.

9. With Blue Sapphire, paint six candles and seven pieces of confetti.

NOTE: Several coats of paint may be needed. Complete one coat over the entire design and allow to dry before painting the next coat. When finished, allow to dry overnight.

Ink:

1. Using the .08 pen, ink the oval border lines and the dots.

2. Using the .05 pen, ink the remainder of the design. ❏

Pattern for Card
(actual size)

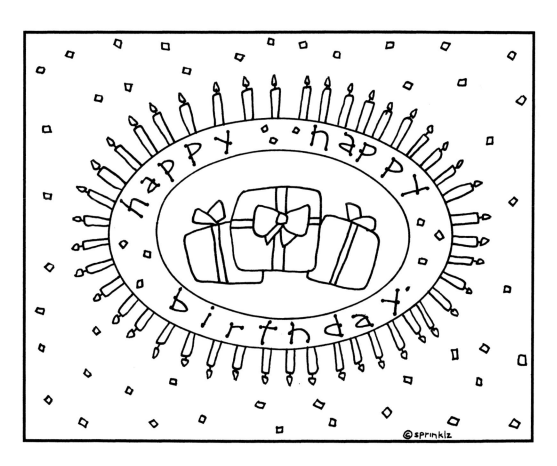

SUPPLIES

Paper:

Cream card stock, 8-1/4" x 10-3/4", 3/4" x 4", and 1-1/2" x 5"

Antique light scrapbook paper, 9-1/2" x 10"

Brown textured paper, 5-1/2" x 6"

White envelope, 4-1/2" x 9-1/2"

Tools & Other Supplies:

12" hemp yarn

2 cream adhesive buttons, 3/4"

8" cream double-face stain ribbon, 1/8" wide

Card stock stickers with dictionary definitions (e.g., "caring," "life," "faith," "special")

Rope border punch

2 white eyelets, 3/8"

Punch and hammer

1-3/4" gold chain

Gold flower charm, 3/4"

1/4" gold jump ring

Glue dots

3 self-adhesive foam mounting squares, 1/4"

Adhesive tape

Quick dry tacky glue

Hole punch, 1/4"

Stylus

Scissors

Ruler

Brown fine tip marker *or* computer and printer

For the inside: Adhesive bandages, ointment, towelette, safety pin, and headache medicine (from your local drugstore)

Patch & Repair
Birthday Card

By Margaret Hanson-Maddox

INSTRUCTIONS

Decorate the Outside:

1. Using the rope border punch, punch along the 8-1/4" edge of the 8-1/4" x 10-3/4" cream card stock.

2. Cut scrapbook paper to 7-3/4" x 9-7/8". Adhere to center of cream card stock.

3. Fold card at 2-3/4" and 6-3/4" from punched edge to form upper flap, middle, and lower flap.

4. From brown paper, cut three pieces: 1-1/4" x 3-3/8", 1-3/8" x 1-1/2", and 5/8" x 5-3/8".

5. From card stock stickers cut out words of your choice and adhere to brown paper pieces, leaving a 1/4" border.

6. On the 1-3/8" x 1-1/2" piece, apply an eyelet in the upper left and upper right corners.

7. Add jump ring to charm and place on chain. Run ends of chain through eyelets and secure with quick dry tacky glue on back side.

58

8. Using foam mounting squares, apply eyelet paper square to lower left area of upper flap.

9. Apply the 1-1/4" x 3-3/8" brown paper to right side of flap. Trim upper left corner as needed.

10. Apply 5/8" x 5-3/8" piece of brown paper to upper area of lower flap.

11. Attach one button at center of upper flap. Align the other button and adhere on lower flap. Glue one end of hemp close to top button.

Decorate the Inside:

1. From antique light scrapbook paper, cut two pieces: 1-5/8" x 4-5/8" and 2" x 5-3/8".

2. From brown paper, cut two pieces: 1" x 4-1/4" and 1" x 4-3/8".

3. Hand print or use your computer to print "You're at the age of patch and repair!" on cream card stock. Cut out a piece of cream card stock 7/8" x 4" with the lettering. Also from cream card stock, cut a piece 1-1/2" x 4-7/8".

4. Glue the 7/8" x 4" cream card stock to the 1" x 4-1/4" brown paper. Glue these to the 1-5/8" x 4-5/8" scrapbook paper. Glue to the top left at a slight angle.

5. Glue the 1" x 4-1/4" brown paper to the 1-1/2" x 4-7/8" cream card stock. Glue these to the 2" x 5-3/8" scrapbook paper. Cut out words from card stock stickers and apply. Glue at center of lower flap.

6. Tie two bows from ribbon. Glue at right upper corners of message rectangles.

7. Using glue dots, adhere medical items to center area of card. Use a 3/8" x 1" piece of cream card stock to apply safety pin.

8. Fold card closed and wrap hemp around buttons in a figure eight to secure flaps.

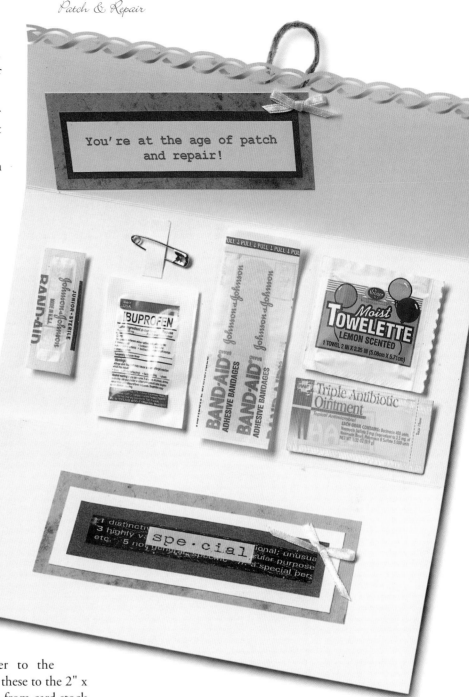

Decorate the Envelope:

1. Cut a 1-5/8" x 1-7/8" of scrapbooking paper. Adhere to lower left corner of envelope, leaving a 1/8" margin.

2. Cut a 3/4" x 5" strip of cream card stock. Glue diagonally to lower left area of envelope. Trim ends.

3. Cut out a word from the card stock stickers. Adhere in center of scrapbooking paper, overlapping the cream card stock strip. ❑

Thank You Cards
&
Get Well Cards

When words alone won't do, create a card to say
"thank you" or to send get-well wishes.
Your personal, colorful creation is a sure way
to brighten someone's day.

SUPPLIES

Paper:

Ivory card with deckle edge,
   5" x 7"

Old postcard with rose motifs

Small checked paper

Adhesive-backed vellum

Tools & Other Supplies:

Clip art images - Roses

Walnut ink and small spray
   bottle

Rubber stamp - Thank you

Ink pad - Gold

1/2 yd. mauve velvet ribbon,
   1/4" wide

Paper adhesive

Scissors

Iron

Paper towels

INSTRUCTIONS

1. Mix walnut ink crystals with water according to manufacturer's instructions. Pour into a small spray bottle. Spray entire card with mixture. Pat dry with paper towels.

2. Tear a piece of checked paper and crumple. Spray with walnut ink mixture. Pat with paper towel. Iron flat.

3. Apply adhesive to the back of the paper. Adhere checked paper to the front of the card.

4. Photocopy old postcard. Apply adhesive to the back of the postcard and adhere to the front of the card covering the check paper.

5. Print clip art on adhesive-backed vellum. Cut printed pieces from the vellum. Adhere printed vellum to the front of the card, slightly overlapping the edges of the postcard.

Roses Collage

Thank You Card

By Rebekah Meier

6. Tie mauve velvet ribbon around the left edge of the front of the card along the fold. Trim ends. ❑

Creative Thank You

Thank You Card

By Rebekah Meier

SUPPLIES

Paper:
Ivory card with deckle edge, 5" x 7"
Paper with writing
Cream mottled paper

Tools & Other Supplies:
Scissors
Heat transfer tool
Clip art - Illuminated letters
Paper adhesive
Walnut ink crystals and small spray bottle
Iron
1/2 yd. brown striped ribbon, 1/4" wide
Computer and laser printer
Paper towels

INSTRUCTIONS

1. Mix walnut ink crystals with water according to manufacturer's instructions. Pour into a small spray bottle. Spray entire card with mixture. Pat dry with paper towel. Let dry. Iron card.

2. Tear a piece of paper with writing. Apply paper adhesive to the back. Adhere to the front upper left section of the card.

3. Print letters (your choice) from clip art on cream mottled paper. Cut out letters and apply paper adhesive to the backs. Adhere the letters to the card.

4. Type CREATE and Thank You on a computer, using the Papyrus font. Reverse the images and print out on a laser printer.

5. Lay the CREATE image face down on the right side of the card. Rub the back of the image with the hot transfer tool. (The image will be transferred to the card.)

6. Transfer the Thank You image to a piece of cream mottled paper, using the same technique. Tear around the words and apply to the lower left of the card.

7. Tie the brown stripe ribbon around the front of the card at the fold. Trim the ends of the ribbon. ❏

SUPPLIES

Paper:

Double-sided blue print card stock, 8-1/2" x 11"

White envelope, 9-1/2" x 4-1/4"

Floral tag

Beige paper, 1-1/4" x 5/8" printed or hand-lettered with "Best Friend"

Tools & Other Supplies:

Diamond border punch

Round corner-edger scissors

Self-adhesive hook-and-loop tape, 3/4" square

Stickers - Flowers, butterfly, dragonfly, ladybugs

Dimensional corners and large pansy stickers

Quick dry tacky glue

Glue dots

Scissors

Ruler

For the inside: Adhesive bandages, safety pin, aspirin, antacid tablets, and/or ointment of your choice (from your local drugstore)

Pansy Medical Kit

Get Well Card

By Margaret Hanson-Maddox

INSTRUCTIONS

Decorate the Outside:

1. Cut double-sided blue print card stock to 8-1/2" x 10".

2. Using the diamond border punch, punch along 8-1/2" edge.

3. Fold card at 2-5/8" and 6-7/8" from punched border to form upper flap, middle, and lower flap.

4. Attach hook side of hook-and-loop tape to upper flap. Align loop piece and adhere to lower flap.

5. Using round corner scissors, round the corners on the lower flap.

6. Add stickers to each corner on lower flap.

7. Attach corner stickers to upper corners on upper flap.

8. Attach flower sticker to center of upper flap.

Decorate the Inside:

1. Attach sticker insects to upper flap.
2. Using glue dots, attach medical packets. Use a 1/2" x 1" piece of card stock to attach safety pin.
3. Attach floral tag to lower flap. Adhere "Best Friend" paper at center of floral sticker.

Decorate Envelope:

1. Cut 1/4" strips of blue printed card stock. Glue diagonally on lower left corner.
2. Apply floral sticker over diagonal strips. ❏

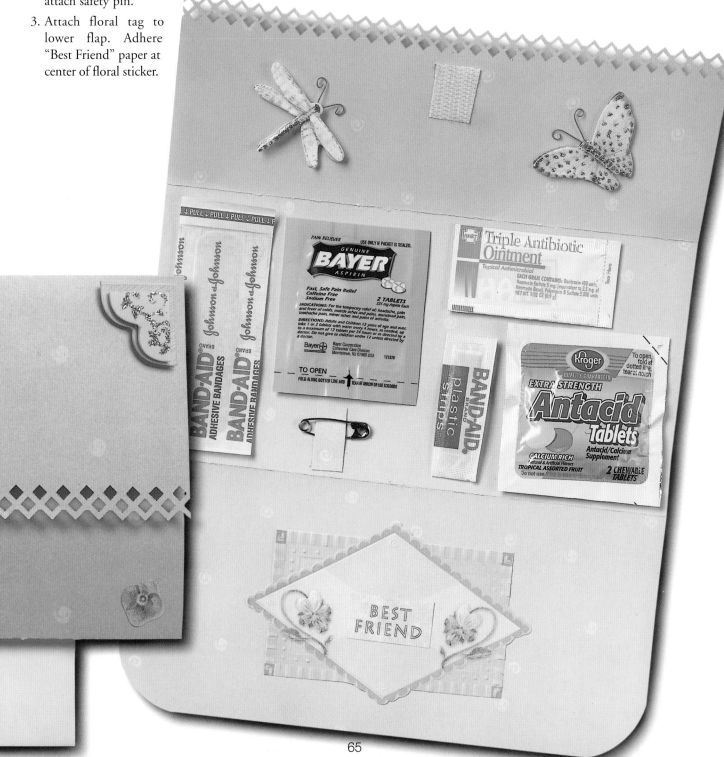

Lily Garland

Get Well Card

By Nancy Hamby

INSTRUCTIONS

1. Stamp the one calla lily motif on the front of the card. Stamp an additional motif on a piece of ivory card stock.
2. Color both with colored pencils.
3. Cut off the bottom of the card front around the stamped motif.
4. Glue a piece of green card stock to the inside of the card.
5. Stamp "Get Well" on the green card stock with gold ink. Emboss with gold powder.
6. Lightly sponge gold and green ink on the front of the card. Sponge gold ink over the green card stock.
7. Cut out the second lily motif. Shape the leaves and flowers slightly to give a dimensional look. Use self-adhesive dots to glue on top of the stamped design on the card.
8. Tie a ribbon bow and glue to the front of the card.
9. Edge the card with gold, using the paint pen. ❏

Best Wishes Butterfly

Get Well Card

By Pat Schreiber

INSTRUCTIONS

1. Fold 5-1/2" x 8-1/2" black card stock in half with the fold at the top to form a card 5-1/2" x 4-1/4".
2. Punch the lower left and right corners of the front of the card with the butterfly punch. Color these small butterflies with a gold pen.
3. Center the decorative paper and glue to the card front.
4. Stamp the butterfly with black pigment ink on black card stock. Cover with black embossing powder and set with an embossing heat gun. Allow to cool.
5. Cut out the butterfly. In each section of the wings, dampen with the blending pen and cover the section with pigment powder using a paintbrush or cotton swab to apply and coloring the butterfly to match the background paper. Rub the completed butterfly to remove any excess powder.
6. Curve wings of butterfly with the handles of the scissors. Apply glue to the bottom of the body and attach to the card at an angle. ❏

SUPPLIES

Paper:

Black card stock, 5-1/2" x 8-1/2" and 4" x 3-1/2"

Jewel-tone decorative paper, 4-1/2" x 3-3/8"

Tools & Other Supplies:

Rubber stamp - Butterfly

Embossing powder - Black

Pigment ink pad - Black

Scissors

Glue stick

Butterfly corner punch

Pigment powders - Rose, gold, pewter, purple, green (to match the decorative paper)

Blender pen

Old small round paintbrush *or* cotton swabs

Gold metallic paint pen

Bon Voyage Cards
&
Wish You Were Here

Whether it's a trip to the beach, a vacation to a foreign
land, or a flight of fancy that's a departure from
everyday routine, there's a card to capture the mood
and mark the moment.

SUPPLIES

Paper:

140 lb. soft press watercolor paper, 11" x 8-1/2" and 6" x 5"

Acrylic Craft Paints:

All are metallic colors.

Amethyst

Inca Gold

Periwinkle

Plum

Sequin Black

Glazing medium

Tools & Other Supplies:

Technical pens with black ink, .05, .08

Artist brushes - #2 round, 3/4" wash

7" 19-gauge wire

Self-adhesive dots, smallest size

Painter's tape

Cellophane tape

Wire cutters

Needlenose pliers

Circle template *or* circle cutter

Scissors

Wet palette *or* foam plate

Tracing paper, transfer paper, and stylus

Kneaded eraser

Pencil and sharpener

Paper towels

Water container

Patterns are found on pages 72 & 73.

Take Flight
Bon Voyage

By Marni Adams

INSTRUCTIONS

Prepare Card:

1. Fold larger piece of watercolor paper in half to create a vertical card 5-1/2" x 8-1/2".

2. Trace pattern and use graphite paper to transfer border lines only. Use a kneaded eraser to erase any mistakes.

Paint the Card Background:

1. Using painter's tape, block off the left panel.

2. Mix equal amounts glazing medium and Periwinkle. Using a 3/4" wash brush, paint left background panel. Remove tape. Allow to dry.

3. Using painter's tape, block off the outer border along the top right, right, and bottom right of the card.

4. Mix equal amounts glazing medium and Amethyst. Using a 3/4" wash brush, paint border. Remove tape. Allow to dry.

5. Using painter's tape, block off the thin vertical stripe.

6. Using the #2 brush with Sequin Black, paint the stripe. Apply additional coats, if necessary. Remove tape. Allow to dry.

Transfer:

1. Using graphite paper, transfer remainder of design to the front of the card.

2. Transfer the butterfly design to the smaller piece of watercolor paper. Use a kneaded eraser to erase any mistakes.

Paint the Card Background Design:

Use the #2 round brush.

1. With Periwinkle, paint one-third of the hearts.

2. With Amethyst, paint another third of the hearts.

3. With Plum, paint the rest of the hearts.

Continued on page 73

May all your dreams take flight

sprinklz

Pattern for Take Flght – Card Front (actual size)

Continued from page 70

4. With Inca Gold, paint the dots.

NOTE: Several coats of paint may be needed. Complete one coat over the entire design and allow to dry before painting the next coat. When finished, allow to dry overnight.

Paint the Butterfly:

Use the #2 round brush. Use the photo as a guide.

1. With Sequin Black, paint the body and wing divisions.

2. With Amethyst, paint the starbursts on the wings.

3. With Plum, paint the hearts on the wings.

4. With Inca Gold, paint the ovals and dots on the wings.

5. With Periwinkle, paint the remaining shapes. See NOTE above. Allow to dry overnight.

Ink:

1. Using the .08 pen, ink the border lines on the card and the outside edge of the butterfly.

2. Using the .05 pen, ink the lettering and the design details on the card and the butterfly. TIP: Use the circle template when inking the dots - 3/32" on the left panel and 7/64" on the rest.

Assemble:

1. Using scissors, carefully cut around the outside edges of the butterfly.

2. Use the stylus to score along the edges of the butterfly's body and gently fold the wings toward the center.

3. Use the needlenose pliers to fold wire in half. Then twist the ends into curlicues to form antennae.

4. Use cellophane tape to attach the antennae to the back of the butterfly.

5. Use self-adhesive dots to attach the butterfly to the front of the card. Use the photo as a guide for placement. ❑

Pattern for Take Flght – Butterfly (actual size)

Instructions begin on page 70.

SUPPLIES

Paper:

Brown card stock, 4" x 5-1/4" and 3" x 3"

Taupe card stock, 8-1/2" x 5-1/2"

Decorative paper with shells and sand, 3-3/4" x 5"

Tools & Other Supplies:

3 small shells

Glue stick

White tacky glue

24" copper and black metal-lic fiber or thin yarn

18" black and cream fiber

1/8" hole punch

INSTRUCTIONS

Construct the Card:

1. Fold the taupe card stock in half, placing the fold on the left side.

2. Center and glue the 4"x 5-1/4" piece of brown card stock on top of the card.

3. Center and glue the shells and sand dec-orative paper on top of the brown card stock.

Make Sandals:

1. Using the pattern provided, cut out two sandals from the 3" square of brown card stock.

Walk on the Beach

Wish You Were Here

By Pat Schreiber

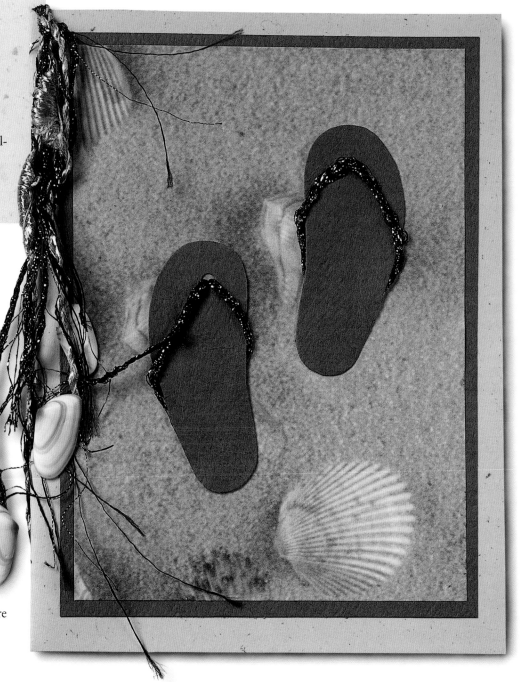

2. Punch a hole in each sandal. (Placement is indicated by the dot on the pattern.)

3. Cut two 3" pieces of copper and black metallic fiber. Fold each 3" piece in half. Push this fold through the hole and glue to the bottom of the sandal.

4. Wrap the loose ends of the fiber pieces to the bottom of each side of one sandal. Glue in place. Repeat this process for the other sandal.

5. Glue sandals on the shells and sand paper as shown.

Finish:

1. Fold the two fiber pieces in half. Open the card and wrap the left side with the fibers. Knot at the top of the card.

2. Glue three small shells with white tacky glue to three ends of the fibers. Allow to dry. ❑

Pattern for Walk on the Beach (actual size)

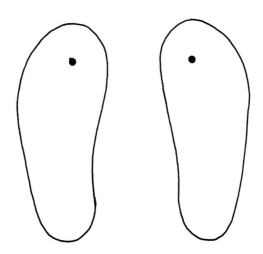

SUPPLIES

Paper:

Foam core board, 4-1/4" x 5-1/2"

1 sheet decorative paper with palm trees and beach scenes

1 acetate sheet

White card stock, 8-1/2" x 5-1/2"

Tools & Other Supplies:

Beach sand

5 tiny shells

1 white medium shell

Glue stick

Double-sided tape, 1/4" wide

14" white cording

White tacky glue

Craft knife

Ruler

Scissors

Sandy Beaches
Wish You Were Here

By Pat Schreiber

INSTRUCTIONS

1. Fold the white card stock in half with the fold on the left side to make a card 4-1/4" x 5-1/2".
2. Draw a rectangle 2-1/4" x 3" on the foam board 1" from the top, 1" from the left and right sides, and 1-1/2" from the bottom edge. Cut out, using a craft knife.
3. Cut a piece of palm tree paper 6" x 7-1/2".
4. Rub the front of the foam board with a glue stick and place, face down, on the center of the back of the beach paper. Smooth in place. Wrap the edges of the card and glue the excess paper to the back of the foam board. Cut an X over the window. Wrap the edges of the rectangle with the paper and glue the excess to the back of foam board. TIP: If any white shows in the corners, color with a dark marker or attach small pieces of paper to hide the exposed foam board.
5. Cut the acetate sheet 2-5/8" x 3-3/8". Place 1/4" double-sided tape on the front of the card around the edges of the window. Be sure the tape does not extend into the opening; the sand you add later will adhere to any exposed tape. Place the acetate sheet on the tape and press to seal. Avoid getting fingerprints on the window.
6. Cut a 3-1/4" x 4-3/4" piece of beach paper that shows both the ocean and the sky. Check to be sure that the ocean and sky will appear through the window. Set aside.
7. Turn over the card and place five tiny shells on the window.
8. Add the about a tablespoon of sand. Leave the card face down.
9. Place double-sided tape on the back of the card around the edges of the window. Be sure the tape does not extend into the opening. Place the beach cutout over the tape and press to seal.
10. Glue the card to the back of the foam board.
11. On the front of the card, place double-sided around the edges of the window. Be sure that the tape does not extend into the window. Adhere the white cording to the tape, overlapping the ends at the lower right corner.
12. With white tacky glue, glue the medium shell over the ends of the cording. ❑

Greetings from Italy

Wish You Were Here

By Barbara Mansfield

INSTRUCTIONS

1. Cut a 1-1/2" x 5" strip of crackled paper.
2. Tear one edge of grape paper to make a piece about 3-3/4" x 5".
3. Tear one edge of brown paper to make a piece about 2-1/4" x 5".
4. Attach papers with double-stick tape with the torn edges overlapping the crackled paper strip.
5. Adhere to card with double-stick tape. Trim edges.
6. Adhere sticker to brown paper part of card.
7. Loop ribbon around folded edge of card. Tie in a bow. ❏

SUPPLIES

Paper:

Cream card, 6-1/2" x 5"

Brown textured paper

Printed paper with grapes

Printed paper with crackled design

Tools & Other Supplies:

Sticker - Canceled Italian postage stamp

2/3 yd, wine satin ribbon, 1/8" wide

Double-stick tape

Scissors

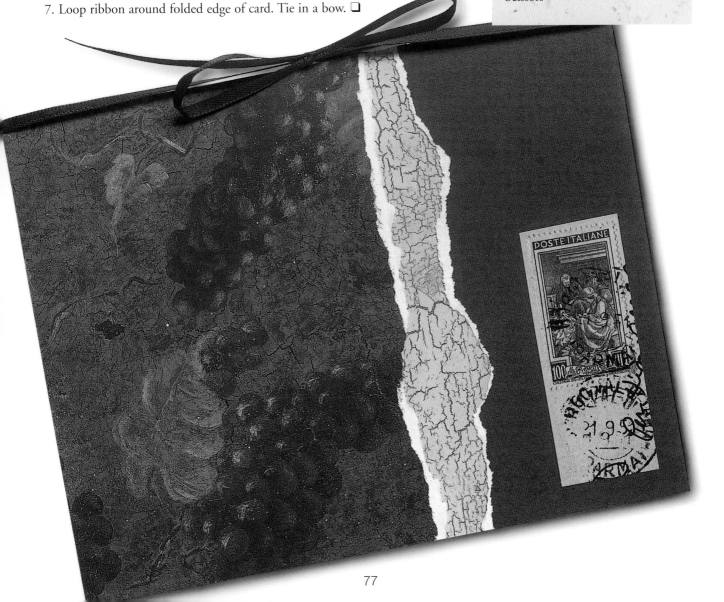

Memories Are Forever
Bon Voyage

SUPPLIES

Paper:

Burgundy card stock

Cream card stock

Green card stock

Decorative paper with script writing

1 sheet white computer paper

Tools & Other Supplies:

Cameo embellishment

Feather

Deckle ruler

White tacky glue

Antique glass coating for paper

Computer and printer

Memories Are Forever
Bon Voyage

By Pat Schreiber

INSTRUCTIONS

Construct the Card:

1. Cut burgundy card stock 8-1/2" x 5-1/2". Fold in half with the fold on the left side to form a card 4-1/4" x 5-1/2".

2. Tear the edges of the script decorative paper to form a rectangle 3-1/2" x 5-1/4". Center and glue to the base card.

3. Tear the edges of the green paper to form a rectangle 2-1/2" x 4-1/2". Center and glue on the script paper.

Decorate:

1. Tear the edges of the burgundy paper to form a rectangle 3-1/2" x 2-1/4".

2. Print "Memories Are Forever" using a font on your computer.

3. Tear the edges of the white sheet containing the greeting to 2-3/4" x 1-3/4". Round the corners and glue to the burgundy paper.

4. Cover the white area with antique glass coating. (May take two coats.) Allow to thoroughly dry overnight.

5. Glue in place on the card.

6. Glue cameo with the white tacky glue to the upper left side.

7. Glue the feather with the white tacky glue across the bottom of the card. ❑

Postmark Travel Card

Wish You Were Here

By Barbara Mansfield

SUPPLIES

Paper:

Cream card, 6-1/2" x 5"

Printed paper with postal motifs, 4-1/2" x 6"

Red mulberry paper

Tools & Other Supplies:

Ink pads for rubber stamping - Medium gray, chocolate

48" off-white fiber or thin yarn

Postmark stickers

4 eyelets

Double-stick tape

Round artist brush

INSTRUCTIONS

1. Apply both stamp pad colors to front of card by lightly rubbing the stamp pad over the surface of the card.

2. Center printed paper on card. Attach with an eyelet in each corner.

3. Use a paint brush to outline a 3" x 5" piece of mulberry paper. Tear on the wet line, pulling the outside paper away. Attach to center of card with double-sided tape.

4. Cut fibers in pieces 3-1/2" to 4-1/2" long. Attach sticker to tops of fibers, then stick at top center of mulberry paper. ❏

Distant Shores

Bon Voyage

By Pat Schreiber

SUPPLIES

Paper:

White card stock, 8-1/2" x 5-1/2"

Blue gingham decorative paper

Red suede paper

Navy card stock, 1-1/2" x 4-1/2"

Purple card stock triangle,
  3-3/4" x 2-3/4"

Tools & Other Supplies:

Crimper

Glue stick

Jewelry glue

Silver ship's wheel or other glue-
  on embellishment

Circle punch, 1-1/2"

Hexagon punch, 1-1/4"

INSTRUCTIONS

1. Fold the white card stock in half placing the fold on the left side to make a card 4-1/4" x 5-1/2".

2. Cut a 5" x 4-1/2" piece of blue gingham decorative paper. Center and glue on the white card.

3. Cut a 3-1/4" x 2-3/4" piece of red suede paper. Glue 1/2" from the top edge of the blue gingham paper.

4. Crimp the navy rectangle. Glue on the red suede paper 1/2" from the left side of the suede paper and 1/8" from the top edge.

5. Glue the purple triangle on the crimped strip.

6. Punch a 1-1/2" circle from blue gingham paper.

7. Punch a hexagon from red suede paper. Glue on the gingham circle.

8. Using jewelry glue, attach the ship's wheel charm on the red suede hexagon.

9. Glue this section to the card as shown. ❏

SUPPLIES

Paper:

Navy card stock, 5-1/2" x 6-1/2", 3-3/4" x 4-1/2"

Medium brown card stock, 3" x 7-1/2"

White card stock, 2-1/2" x 2-3/4"

Decorative paper with map motifs, 4-3/4" x 5-3/4"

Tools & Other Supplies:

Large round corner punch

Rubber stamps - Sailboat, greeting of your choice

Dye-based ink pads - Black, navy

Artist chalk - Pale blue, medium blue, medium brown

Cotton balls

Glue stick

INSTRUCTIONS

1. Fold the medium brown card stock in half to make a 3" x 3-3/4" card with the fold at the top.

2. Open the brown card and stamp the greeting on the inside with navy ink. Allow to dry.

3. Close the card. Rub the edge of the card with the navy ink pad.

4. Stamp the sailboat on the white card stock with black ink. Allow to dry. Using a cotton ball, color the sky with light blue chalk. Color the base of the boat with medium brown chalk and the sea with the medium blue chalk.

5. Using the large round corner punch, round the corners for the 3-3/4" x 4-1/2" navy card stock, the 3" x 3-3/4" medium brown card stock, the 2-1/2" x 2-3/4" white card stock, and the 4-3/4" x 5-3/4" map decorative paper.

6. Center and glue the map to the 5-1/2" x 6-1/2" navy card stock. Center and glue the 3-3/4" x 4-1/2" navy card stock to the map. Center and glue the medium brown card with the greeting to the blue card stock. Center and glue the white card stock to the brown card. ❑

Sailboat Surprise

Bon Voyage

By Pat Schreiber

Cards for Any Occasion

Send a special message, extend an invitation, evoke a mood, or say you care with a card. At the end of this section, you'll see how to make an envelope folder that can be customized to hold a card of any size.

SUPPLIES

Paper:

140 lb. soft press watercolor paper, 8-1/2" x 5-1/2"

Tools & Other Supplies:

Set of artist chalks (24 colors)

Technical pens with black ink, .05, .08

Artist brush - #2 round

Cotton swabs

Kneaded eraser

Tracing paper, graphite transfer paper

Stylus

Pencil and sharpener

Ruler

Scissors *or* paper cutter

Paper towels

Water container

INSTRUCTIONS

Fold & Ink:

1. Fold watercolor paper in half to create vertical card 4-1/4" x 5-1/2".

2. Trace pattern. Using graphite transfer paper, transfer design to front of card. Use a kneaded eraser to erase any mistakes.

3. Using the .08 pen, ink the banner and the dots.

4. Using the .05 pen, ink the remainder of the design.

You Are an Angel

By Marni Adams

Color with Chalk:

1. Using light blue and violet, apply color to the background with damp cotton swabs.

2. Use a dampened #2 brush to apply:

   • Red to the hearts with wings and the hearts on the apron.

   • Ruddy red to the background hearts and the hearts on the banner.

   • Yellow, to the stars with wings, the stars on the apron, and the stars in the angel's hair.

   • Yellow orange, to the background stars and the edges of the banner.

   • Royal blue, to the dress (leaving the ruffles white) and the edges of the wings.

   • Violet, to the squares on the apron and the border around the large heart on the apron.

   • Light blue, to the edges of the apron.

   • Flesh, to the angel's face, neck, and feet.

   • Light brown, to the hair.

   • Pink, to the angel's cheeks. ❏

Pattern for Card
(actual size)

SUPPLIES

Paper:

140 lb. soft press watercolor
paper, 8-1/2" x 11"

Watercolor Pencils:

Canary Yellow

Crimson Red

Grass Green

Blue

Poppy Red

Sunburst Yellow

True Blue

True Green

Tools & Other Supplies:

Technical pens with black ink,
.01, .05, .08

Artist brushes - #2 round, #6
round

Tracing paper, graphite transfer
paper, stylus

Kneaded eraser

Pencil and sharpener

Ruler

Paper towels

Water container

Singing Your Praises

By Marni Adams

Pattern for Card
(Enlarge @125% for actual size)

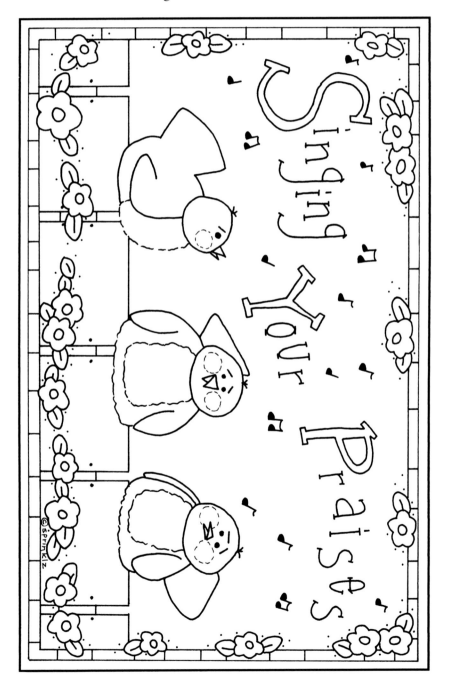

INSTRUCTIONS

Prepare Card:

1. Fold watercolor paper to create horizontal card 8-1/2" x 5-1/2".

2. Trace pattern and transfer design to front of card. Use a kneaded eraser to erase any mistakes.

Color:

1. With Blue, color the background, leaving the fence white.

2. With Canary Yellow, color the birds' bellies and the flower petals.

3. With Poppy Red, color the birds' cheeks and the flower centers.

4. With Crimson Red, color the letter "S," the bird on the left, and alternating inner border segments.

5. With Sunburst Yellow, color the letter "Y," the center bird, and the birds' beaks.

6. With True Blue, color the letter "P," the bird on the right, and remaining inner border segments.

7. With True Green, color half the leaves.

8. With Grass Green, color the remaining leaves and the outer border.

9. Wet colored areas with a brush dampened with water. Allow to dry overnight. TIPS: Every time you put the brush in water, blot it on a paper towel. Rinse thoroughly between colors. Use the #6 brush for larger areas and the #2 brush for smaller areas.

Ink:

1. Using the .01 pen, ink the cheek outlines.

2. Using the .08 pen, ink the nails on the fence.

3. Using the .05 pen, ink the remainder of the design and the dots. ❏

SUPPLIES

Paper:

White card stock, 6-1/8" x 6-7/8" (for card) and 6" x 8"

Green paper, 3/4" x 1"

White envelope, 3-5/8" x 6-3/8"

Paints:

Dimensional paper paints - Red, Yellow

Acrylic craft paints - Light Cinnamon, Khaki Tan, Buttermilk

Tools & Other Supplies:

Dye ink pads - Red, blue

Rubber stamp - "You're Invited"

Cellulose household sponge, 2" x 2"

Stencils - 1/4" checks, caption bubbles

Black marker, .03

Black colored pencil

2 woodlet circles, 1-1/4"

Black craft foam sheet, 1-1/4" circle

Yellow craft foam sheet, 1" square

Artist brush - #4 round

Palette or foam plate

Water basin

Paper towels

Crimper

Self-adhesive foam squares or dots, 1/2"

Hot glue gun and glue stick

Tacky glue

Glue stick

Pencil

Scissors

Ruler

Tracing paper, transfer paper, and stylus

Ant pattern

Picnic Invitation

By Margaret Hanson-Maddox

INSTRUCTIONS

Refer to the photograph frequently for details and placement.

Decorate the Outside:

1. Fold the larger piece of white card stock to measure 3-7/16" x 6-7/8" when folded.

2. Position checks stencil on front of card. Tap sponge on red dye ink pad and tap over stencil. Let dry. Reposition stencil to continue for complete coverage of card front.

3. Using the caption bubbles stencil, trace two bubbles on white card stock. Cut out. Using the black marker, print "Picnic!" on one and "Food! Fun" on the other. Add broken stitch lines around each caption bubble.

4. Using adhesive squares or dots, apply caption bubbles to card.

5. Using a pencil, trace ant pattern onto tracing paper. Transfer ants to front of card using transfer paper and a stylus.

5. Using the black colored pencil, color each ant. Lightly shade the left side of each body.

6. Using the black marker, add legs to each ant.

Picnic Invitation, continued

Decorate the Inside:

1. Position check stencil on lower edge of card. Tap sponge on red dye ink pad and tap over two rows only. Let dry.

2. Tap rubber stamp on blue dye ink pad and stamp "You're Invited" 2-1/4" from left edge of card.

3. Using the caption bubbles stencil, trace one bubble on remaining white card stock and cut out. Using the black marker, print "Come Join Us!" in center of caption bubble. Add broken stitch lines around bubble.

Make the Hamburger:

1. Using hot glue gun and glue stick, dot on "sesame seeds" on one side of one round wood piece.

2. Paint both round wood pieces with Khaki Tan.

3. Lightly add Light Cinnamon to left side of each "sesame seed".

4. Paint "sesame seeds" with Buttermilk.

5. Run green paper through crimper.

6. Glue one round wood piece (the one without "sesame seeds") to left of "You're Invited."

7. Glue round black foam piece (hamburger patty) on round wood piece.

8. Glue yellow square foam (cheese) on black foam.

9. Glue green crimped paper (lettuce) on yellow foam.

10. Drizzle yellow (mustard) and red (ketchup) dimensional paints over "lettuce." Place remaining round wood piece on the wet paint. Be sure the "sesame seeds" side is up. Let dry completely.

Decorate the Envelope:

1. Position the check stencil on the left edge of the envelope.

2. Tap sponge on red dye ink pad and tap over two rows only. Let dry.

3. Following instructions previously, add three ants.

4. Sponge red checks on envelope flap. Add four ants. ❏

SUPPLIES

Paper:

Cream card, 6-1/2" x 5"

Decoupage paper, dragonfly motif

Green striped paper

Tools & Other Supplies:

Diamond border punch

Double-stick tape

Scissors *or* craft knife

INSTRUCTIONS

1. Punch long edge of card with border punch.

2. Cut a 1" x 6-1/2" strip of green striped paper - get as much green as possible. Adhere to inside front cover under punched border with green showing.

3. Cut 5-1/2" x 3-3/4" from striped paper with green stripes at both short ends. Center on card and adhere.

4. Cut out dragonfly to make a paper panel 2-1/2" x 2-1/4". Adhere at center of striped paper. ❏

By Barbara Mansfield

Paper:

Cream card, 6-1/2" x 5"

Brown decoupage paper with leaf motifs

Green background paper with script writing

Tools & Other Supplies:

Scissors *or* craft knife

12" each of 12 different fibers or yarn

2 green skeleton leaves

Double-stick tape

Glue

Leaves & Fibers

By Barbara Mansfield

INSTRUCTIONS

1. Cut a piece of brown paper 4-1/2" x 6".

2. Cut green paper 4" x 5-1/2". Center on brown and attach with double-stick tape.

3. Attach papers to center of card with double-stick tape.

4. Loosely tie fibers in single knot.

5. Glue leaves as pictured. Glue fiber knot to stem ends of leaves. ❏

Tea for Two

By Nancy Hamby

INSTRUCTIONS

1. Cut a piece of plaid paper the size of the card and glue to the front.

2. Using the template, cut out a circle 3-1/8" from the card front.

SUPPLIES

Paper:

Ivory card, 5" x 6-1/2"

Blue and yellow plaid paper

Ivory card stock

Blue card stock

Tools & Other Supplies:

Rubber stamps - Herbal tea, "Tea for Two," teacups, teapot, creamer, sugar bowl

Colored pencils

Permanent ink - Black

Self-adhesive dimensional dots

5 blue eyelets

Gold paint pen

Circle cutter template set

Craft knife and cutting mat

3. Edge the circle and the card front with the gold pen.

4. Stamp all the designs on ivory card stock. Color with pencils.

5. Cut the words in a rectangle. Glue to a piece of blue card stock to make a border, and edge with the gold pen. Place an eyelet in each corner.

6. Cut the herbal tea stamp in the shape of a tag. Glue to a piece of blue card stock and trim. Attach the tag to the card with an eyelet.

7. Use self-adhesive dots to attach the words, using the photo as a guide.

8. Cut out the cups, creamer, and sugar bowl and glue to the front of the card.

9. Using a template, draw a circle 3-3/4" around the stamped teapot. Glue inside the card so the teapot shows through the cutout circle. ❑

SUPPLIES

Paper:

White card, 6-1/4" square

Yellow gold card stock

Maroon card stock

White card stock

Tools & Other Supplies:

Rubber stamp - Flower tiles

Colored pencils

Permanent ink - Black

Pigment Inks - Green, yellow gold, purple, maroon

Clear embossing ink

Clear embossing powder

Maroon fine tip marker

29 black eyelets

8 maroon eyelets

Paper glue

1 yd. yarn

Cosmetic sponge *or* stencil brush

Craft knife and cutting mat

Wildflowers

By Nancy Hamby

INSTRUCTIONS

1. Stamp the tile stamp with black ink onto white card stock.

2. Loosely color the design with pencils.

3. Using a cosmetic sponge or stencil brush loaded with pigment inks, scrub color all over the design. Let dry.

4. Apply clear embossing ink to the design. Emboss with clear embossing powder.

5. Cut out the squares and glue to a piece of yellow gold card stock.

6. Place eyelets around all squares as shown.

7. Glue to a piece of maroon card stock and trim.

8. Sponge all the ink colors over the card front and on the envelope flap. Allow to dry.

9. Place a black eyelet in each corner of the card. Place a maroon eyelet on each side of the black corner eyelets.

10. Glue the stamped design in the center of the card.

11. Weave the yarn in and out of the maroon eyelets, tying the bow on the side with the fold.

12. Add lines on the envelope flap with a maroon marker. ❏

Sunflowers

By Nancy Hamby

INSTRUCTIONS

1. Stamp sunflowers motif with black ink on a piece of ivory card stock.

2. Color with pencils.

3. Cut out the motif. Glue to a piece of yellow patterned paper. Cut out to form a border. Glue to the front of the card.

4. Use a craft knife to cut away the background from around the sunflowers and leaves.

5. Adhere a piece of sticky paper to the back of the design on the inside of the card. Drop tiny beads on the sticky paper.

6. Remove the backing from the other side of the sticky paper. Cut a piece of yellow vellum and press over sticky paper.

7. Edge the yellow panel with a green marker.

8. Edge the card with the gold paint pen. ❑

SUPPLIES

Paper:
Ivory card, 5" x 6-1/2"
Ivory card stock
Yellow patterned paper
Yellow vellum
2-sided adhesive paper

Tools & Other Supplies:
Rubber stamp - Sunflower
Permanent ink - Black
Colored pencils
Gold paint pen
Fine-tip green marker
Tiny beads - Green, gold
Scissors
Glue
Craft knife and cutting mat

We Remember Moments

By Nancy Hamby

INSTRUCTIONS

Decorate the Card Front:

1. Stamp the still life design with black ink on a piece of ivory card stock. Let dry.

2. Color with colored pencils and cut out the design.

3. Trim 1-1/4" off the bottom of the front of the card.

4. Cut a piece of blue patterned paper smaller than the remaining front area and glue down.

5. Cut a piece of orange striped paper slightly smaller than the blue patterned paper and glue on top. Place eyelets in corners.

6. Glue the stamped and colored design on top as shown so it extends to the bottom of the card.

Decorate the Inside:

1. Cut a piece of blue card stock to fit the inside of the card. Glue in place.

2. Stamp the words with black ink on ivory card stock. Use an orange marker to draw a narrow border. Cut out.

3. Glue to orange striped paper to make a border, then to blue patterned paper to make a wider border.

4. Glue to the inside of the card. Use a blue marker to draw a narrow border.

Decorate the Envelope:

1. Line the inside of the envelope with the orange striped paper.

2. Stamp the words on ivory card stock. Line with the orange marker. Cut out.

3. Glue to blue card stock, then blue patterned paper to add borders. Glue to the inside of the flap. ❏

Dragonflies

By Nancy Hamby

INSTRUCTIONS

1. Stamp the dragonfly scene twice with black ink on white card stock.
2. Color one entire motif and only one additional dragonfly with colored pastel pencils. TIP: You do not have to color neatly – you can use a paper stump or cotton swab to blend the colors.
3. Apply clear paper paint to the flowers and the dragonfly bodies. Let dry. Apply glitter paper paint to the dragonfly wings. Let dry.
4. Cut out the colored rectangular scene. Cut out the single dragonfly.
5. Glue the rectangular scene to a piece of pink card stock. Cut out pink card stock arond scene, leaving a pink border. Glue pink rectangle to purple paper and cut out, leaving a narrow purple border.

SUPPLIES

Paper:

White card, 5" x 6-1/2"

White envelope

White card stock

Pink card stock

Purple patterned paper

Tools & Other Supplies:

Rubber stamp - Dragonflies and water lilies

Permanent ink - Black

Pigment inks - Lavender, pink, yellow

Silver paint pen

Purple fine-tip marker

Colored pastel pencils

Paper stump *or* cotton swabs

Dimensional paper paints - Clear, glitter

Artist brush

Cosmetic sponge *or* stencil brush

Glue

Craft knife and cutting mat

6. Use a sponge or stencil brush loaded with the yellow, pink, and lavender inks to rub color over the front of the card. Allow to dry.
7. Glue the dragonfly panel to the card front.
8. Cut corners of purple paper and glue in place on card front. Use a purple maker to draw lines to connect the corners and create a line border.
9. Glue a piece of purple paper to the envelope flap. Glue the remaining colored butterfly on the flap. Edge the flap with silver paint. ❑

SUPPLIES

Paper:

White card, 5" x 6-1/2"

White envelope, 7-1/4" x 5-1/4"

White card stock

Green patterned paper

Pink patterned paper

Vellum

Gold metallic woven fiber paper

Tools & Other Supplies:

Rubber stamp - Rose bouquet,
  message words

Permanent ink pad - Black

Pigment ink pad - Gold

Embossing powder - Gold

Watercolor pencils

Small artist brush

8 gold eyelets

Sheer rose ribbon, 1/4" wide

Hole punch

Natural sponge

Glue

Ruler

Craft knife and cutting mat

Yesterday, Today, Tomorrow

By Nancy Hamby

INSTRUCTIONS

Decorate the Cards:

1. Stamp the rose on white card stock with black permanent ink. Let dry.

2. Color the design with watercolor pencils. Use a wet brush to blend the colors, giving a watercolor look.

3. Cut out the motif in a rectangle measuring 3-3/8" x 4-1/4". Edge in gold ink and lightly sponge all over the piece with gold ink.

4. Glue rectangle to a piece of green patterned paper 3/8" larger on all sides. Edge in gold ink and place gold eyelets in corners.

5. Cut a piece of pink patterned paper slightly smaller than the card and glue on the front.

6. Cut the gold woven fiber paper to the same size as the pink paper and glue on top, placing glue where the stamped panel will be. Glue stamped panel on top.

7. Stamp the words on vellum using gold pigment ink. Emboss with gold powder. Cut out to 2-1/4" x 2". Use eyelets to attach the vellum at the bottom of the card.

8. Punch a hole on each side of the vellum and pull up ribbon from behind. Knot each end.

Decorate the Envelope:

1. Cut a piece of pink patterned paper to line the envelope. Edge lining with gold ink. Glue in place.

2. Outline envelope with gold ink. Lightly sponge envelope with gold ink. ❑

Butterfly Greetings

By Nancy Hamby

SUPPLIES

Paper:
White card, 5" x 6-1/2"
White envelope
Yellow card stock
Pink card stock
White card stock

Tools & Other Supplies:
Permanent ink pad - Black
Pigment inks - Yellow, pink, lavender
Metallic ink - Gold
Rubber stamp - Butterfly
Paper paint - Yellow
Colored pencils
14" sheer multi-color ribbon, 1" wide
Butterfly charm
4 pink eyelets
Gold paint pen
Self-adhesive dots
Paper glue
Thin gold cord
Fine-tip markers - Pink, orange
Natural sponge
Paper tape, 3/4" wide
Artist brush
Stencil brush
Ruler
Craft knife and cutting mat

INSTRUCTIONS

Paint & Sponge:
1. Use paper tape to tape off stripes on the front of the card and the envelope flap.
2. Paint with yellow paper paint. Pull off tape.
3. Between stripes, use all three colors of pigment inks and a stencil brush to scrub color randomly.
4. Sponge gold metallic ink on top of the inked stripes. Wipe off ink from yellow stripes.
5. Cut an opening on the card front to fit your butterfly stamp.
6. Use the gold paint pen to edge the outside of the card, the inside of the opening, and the edges of the envelope flap.

Stamp & Color:
1. Stamp the butterfly three times with black ink on white card stock.
2. Color all three butterflies with colored pencils.
3. Cut out a rectangle around one butterfly and mount on pink card stock and cut a rectangle, allowing a pink border. Mount pink rectangle to yellow card stock and cut out, allowing a yellow border. Glue inside the card behind the opening.
4. Cut out the second butterfly. Adhere over the first butterfly with self-adhesive dots.

Embellish:
1. Place eyelets in the corners of the cutout area on the card front.
2. Punch two holes close together under the cutout. Thread ribbon through holes and tie in a bow.
3. Thread gold cord through holes and add charm. Tie in a bow.
4. Glue the remaining butterfly to the envelope flap. Use orange and pink markers to add lines around the edges of the envelope. ❏

SUPPLIES

Paper:

Lime green card stock,
  8-1/2" x 5-1/2"

Hot pink card stock, 3-3/4" x 5"

Pale pink card stock, 2" x 3"

Black card stock

White card stock

Tools & Other Supplies:

Rubber stamps - Music notes,
  music-theme background

Dye-based ink pad - Black

Watermark ink pad

Coffee stirrer

Glue stick

White tacky glue

Circle punches - 3/4", 1-1/4"

Snow texture medium

Paper paint - Red, clear glass
  finish

Palette knife

Back to the 50's

By Pat Schreiber

INSTRUCTIONS

1. Fold the lime green card stock in half with the fold on the left side to make a card 4-1/4" x 5-1/2".
2. Stamp the music background design on the hot pink card stock with watermark ink. Center and glue the hot pink card on the base card.
3. Using a pencil, lightly trace around the glass pattern on the hot pink card stock. Trace the milkshake filling on the pale pink card stock. Cut out and glue on top of the glass outline.
4. Cover the entire glass outline with glass finish paint. Allow to dry.
5. Cut a 1" piece of the coffee stirrer. Glue to the left side of the glass.
6. Apply snow medium using a palette knife so it looks like whipped cream, complete with drips over the edge of the glass. Allow to dry.
7. Paint a red circle at the top center edge of the whipped cream to form the cherry.
8. Punch two large circles from black card stock. Punch two small circles from white card stock.
9. Stamp music notes on the white circles with black ink.
10. Glue the white circles at the centers of the black circles to form records. Overlap the records and glue to the lower right corner of the card. ❑

Pattern for Glass
(Enlarge @200% for actual size)

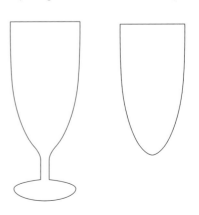

Dancing Shoe

By Pat Schreiber

INSTRUCTIONS

1. Fold black card stock in half, placing the fold at the top of the card, to form a card 5-1/2" x 4-1/4".

2. Center and glue the black and white card stock on the card front.

3. Trace high heel shoe on the pink card stock and cut out. Outline the shoe and detail with the fine black marker. Refer to the pattern for line placement.

4. Cover the outside area of the shoe with the glitter glue. Sprinkle with red glitter. Cover with a sheet of paper and press glitter in place. Remove paper and lightly tap the shoe on the paper to remove excess glitter. Allow to dry.

5. Glue the shoe to the center of the card.

6. Tie a bow with the red organdy ribbon. Slide the stems of the rosebuds through the back of the knot for the bow. Glue in place at the upper right hand corner. ❏

SUPPLIES

Paper:

Black card stock, 5-1/2" x 8-1/2"

Black and white checked floor card stock, 5-1/4" x 4"

Pink card stock

1 sheet copy paper

Tools & Other Supplies:

Red glitter

Glitter glue

2 tiny red rosebuds

12" red sheer ribbon, 7/8" wide

Glue stick

White tacky glue

Scissors

Black fine-tip permanent marker

Tracing paper, transfer paper, and stylus

Pattern for Shoe
(Enlarge @200%
for actual size)

Paper:

Handmade floral paper,
4-1/4" x 5-1/2"

Yellow card stock,
8-1/2" x 5-1/2"

Purple card stock, 3-3/4" x 5"

Tools & Other Supplies:

5 dried violas

3 pieces dried fern

Glue stick

White tacky glue *or* decoupage
medium

Deckle scissors *or* ruler

INSTRUCTIONS

1. Fold the yellow card stock in half, placing the fold on the left side of card.

2. Center and glue the 3-3/4" x 5" purple card stock on the card front.

3. Trim the handmade floral paper with deckle scissors or tear with a ruler to measure 3-1/2" x 4-3/4". Glue to the center of the purple section.

4. Angle and adhere the dried fern pieces to the center of the card. Adhere four violas in a cluster, then adhere the remaining viola to the center of the floral arrangement. ❏

From My Garden
By Pat Schreiber

Simple Violets

By Pat Schreiber

SUPPLIES

Paper:

Floral handmade paper,
4-1/4" x 5-1/2"

Off-white card stock,
8-1/2" x 5-1/2"

Purple mulberry paper

Tools & Other Supplies:

6 dried violas

Dried fern

Glue stick

White tacky glue *or* decoupage
medium

Small self-adhesive dots

INSTRUCTIONS

1. Fold the off-white card stock in half, placing the fold on the left side.

2. Center and glue the handmade paper on the card front.

3. Cut a 2" x 5-1/2" strip of mulberry paper. Lightly moisten the right side of the strip. Gently tear 1/2" off the right side, leaving a strip about 1-1/2" x 5-1/2". Let dry. Glue on the left side of the card, using a glue stick.

4. Glue the dried fern to the center of the card. Adhere three violas, using the photo as a guide for placement. Adhere remaining three violas with self-adhesive dots to give a raised look.

5. Apply a light coat of decoupage medium over the ferns and violas to protect them (especially the ones that are raised). ❏

SUPPLIES

Paper:

Black card stock, 8-1/2" X 5-1/2"

Red card stock, 3" x 4-1/4"

Black suede paper, 2-1/2" x 3-1/2"

Tools & Other Supplies:

1 bamboo skewer

Glue stick

Tacky white glue

Oriental punch with good luck symbol

Acrylic craft paint - Gold metallic

Artist brush

18" thin gold cord

18" gold and black fiber cord

18" black fiber cord

Gold paint pen

INSTRUCTIONS

1. Fold black card stock in half with the fold on the left side of the card.

2. Edge the red card stock with the gold paint pen. Glue to the center of the black card.

3. Punch "good luck" symbols 1/2" from the top and bottom edges of the suede paper. Center and glue on top of the red card stock.

4. Cut the skewer to 4-3/4". Paint with gold metallic paint. Allow to dry.

5. Wrap the painted skewer with the three cords, allowing 3-1/2" of the cords to hang freely at the top. Tie a knot the top of the skewer and wrap 4" downward. Tie off at the bottom and trim to desired length.

6. Glue the wrapped skewer 1/2" from the left side of the card. ❏

Asian Good Luck

By Pat Schreiber

Golden Fan

By Pat Schreiber

INSTRUCTIONS

1. Fold black card stock in half with the fold on the left side of card.

2. Place the deckle ruler on top of the scrap paper, connecting the upper left corner to the lower right corner diagonally. Tear the paper from the upper left corner to the lower right corner. (Both pieces of the paper will be used.)

3. Place the upper half of the scrap paper over the upper half of the card. Using the script stamp with gold ink, fill the lower half of the card with script lines.

SUPPLIES

Paper:

Black card stock, 8-1/2" x 5-1/2"

Scrap paper, 4-1/4" x 5-1/2"

Small piece black card stock

Tools & Other Supplies:

Rubber stamps - Script, oriental fan

Pigment ink pad - Gold metallic

Gold embossing powder

Heat gun for embossing

2 gold beads, 18mm

Self-adhesive foam dots

Deckle ruler

20" beige and black fibers

20" black suede yarn

20" Gold cord

20" Copper and black cord

Metallic rubs - Silver, copper, gold

Scissors

Optional: Cosmetic sponge *or* cotton ball

4. Place the lower half of the scrap paper over the lower half of the card to protect the stamping. Using the three metallic rubs, randomly fill the upper half of the card with metallic colors. Apply with your fingers, a cosmetic sponge, or a cotton ball.

5. On a separate piece of card stock, stamp the fan design with gold ink. Cover the fan with gold embossing powder and set with a heat gun. When cool, cut out the fan shape.

6. Mount the fan cutout at an angle, using self-adhesive dots.

7. Open the card. Wrap the fold of the card with the fibers. Knot at the top of the card.

8. Attach two gold beads at the ends of the dangling fibers. ❑

Love & Hearts

By Karen Embry

INSTRUCTIONS

Paint:

1. Transfer the heart pattern (seven of them) to the watercolor paper.

2. Paint each heart with Baby Pink. Float the right side of each heart with a mix of equal amounts of Baby Pink + Engine Red. Let dry. TIP: Add a little flow medium to the paint when floating - it thins the paint and extends the drying time.

3. Cut out each heart, leaving a thin white border around the edge.

Cut:

1. Cut a piece of white card stock 10-1/8" x 6-7/8". Fold in half.

2. Cut a piece of dark pink card stock 4-5/8" x 6-3/8".

3. Cut a piece of light pink card stock 5" x 4-3/8".

4. Cut a piece of white card stock 3-3/4" x 4-5/8".

Assemble:

1. Center the piece of dark pink card stock on to the front of the card.

2. Center the light pink piece of card stock in the center bottom of the dark pink piece.

3. Center the white piece of card stock in the center of the light pink card stock.

4. Transfer the words "Love" and "You" to the white card stock. Go over the transferred words with the scrapbook marker.

5. Place the flower-shaped brad in the center of the white card stock.

6. Place the self-adhesive dots on the bottoms of six of the heart cutouts. Place the hearts between the words.

7. Glue the beaded fringe to the top edge of the dark pink card stock.

8. Paint tiny dots around the edge of the card and between the tips of the hearts with the Sterling Silver.

9. Glue the remaining heart cutout to the envelope. ❑

Pattern for Card Center (actual size)

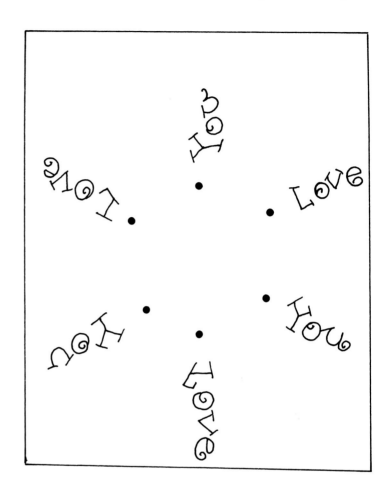

Envelope design

SUPPLIES

Heavy paper or card stock,
  14" x 17"

2 metal eyelets, 3/16"

Small hole punch

24" ribbon, 1/4" wide

Craft knife and cutting mat

Straight edge ruler

Bone folder

This envelope folder can be made any size to fit
the contents - simply measure the card you want to
place inside an envelope and use those measurements
to determine the fold lines on the pattern.
Add flaps of a corresponding size.

INSTRUCTIONS

1. Enlarge pattern to size needed or draw your own pattern to fit the contents.

2. Transfer pattern to heavy paper or card stock.

3. Cut out, using the craft knife and straight edge. Score on fold lines.

4. Use hole punch to punch holes for ribbon where shown on pattern.

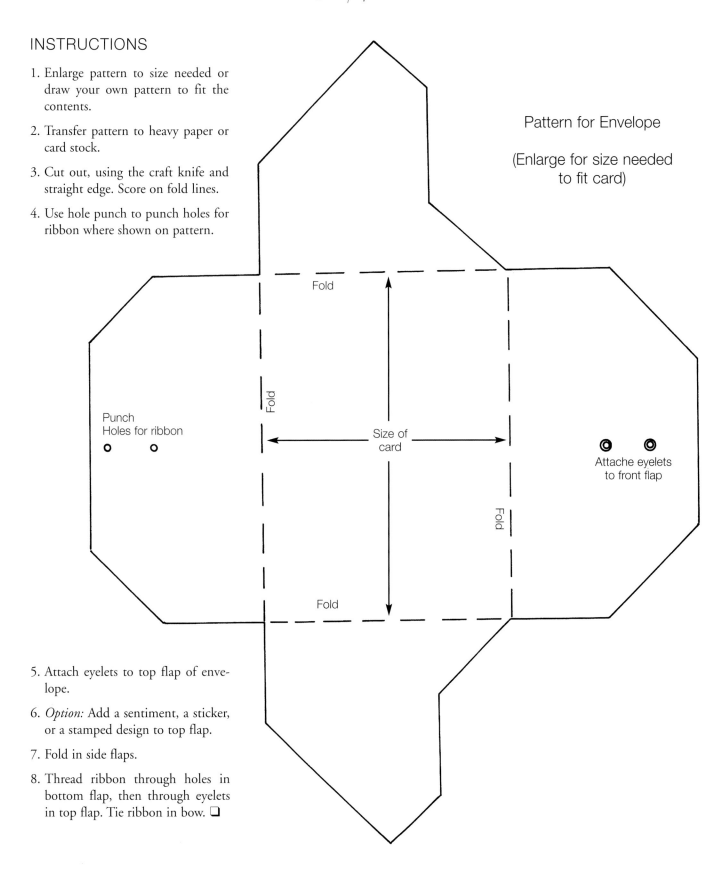

Pattern for Envelope

(Enlarge for size needed to fit card)

Fold

Fold

Punch
Holes for ribbon

Size of
card

Fold

Attache eyelets
to front flap

Fold

5. Attach eyelets to top flap of envelope.

6. *Option:* Add a sentiment, a sticker, or a stamped design to top flap.

7. Fold in side flaps.

8. Thread ribbon through holes in bottom flap, then through eyelets in top flap. Tie ribbon in bow. ❑

Holiday Cards

Holidays are traditional times for sending cards. Why not
make the cards you send and start a new holiday tradition?
In this section, you'll find great seasonal delights to
send to your friends.

SUPPLIES

Paper:

Purple card stock, 10" x 6-7/8", folded in half

White card stock, 4" x 5-7/8" and 3/8" x 4"

White 140-lb. watercolor paper, 3-5/8" x 5-5/8"

White envelope, 7-1/4" x 5-1/4"

Paper Paints:

Amethyst (metallic)

Baby Pink

Berry Wine

Blue Sapphire (metallic)

Calypso Sky

Dioxazine Purple

Engine Red

Licorice

Pumpkin Orange

School Bus Yellow

Flow medium (to thin the paint for stroke work)

Other Supplies & Tools:

Black permanent fine point scrapbook marker

16" narrow white rick-rack trim

5 flower-shaped brads, 1/2" - 1 purple, 2 pink, 1 yellow, 1 blue

2 flower-shaped brads, 1/4" - purple

Paper trimmer

Artist brushes - # 4 round, 1/4" angled shader

Tacky glue

Glue stick

Tracing paper, transfer paper, stylus

Happy Easter

By Karen Embry

INSTRUCTIONS

Paint:

1. Transfer the animals and bugs design to the watercolor paper.

2. Paint the chick with School Bus Yellow. Float the bottom edge with Pumpkin Orange. Paint the beak with Pumpkin Orange.

3. Paint the area around the chick with a mix of equal amounts flow medium + Calypso Blue.

4. Paint the bunny with Baby Pink. Float the bottom edge of the bunny body with a mix of Engine Red + Baby Pink. Paint the nose and inside the ears with this mix. Paint the area around the bunny with a mix of equal amounts of flow medium + Amethyst.

5. Paint the butterfly body with a mix of Amethyst + Wicker White. Float the bottom edge of the body with Dioxazine Purple. Paint the wings with Calypso Blue. Float the bottom edge with Blue Sapphire. Paint the area around the butterfly with a mix of equal amounts flow medium + Baby Pink.

6. Paint the ladybug with Engine Red. Float the bottom of the ladybug's body with Berry Wine. Paint the ladybug's head and dots with Licorice. Paint the area outside the ladybug with a mix of equal amounts flow medium + School Bus Yellow.

7. Paint a coordinating chick (or other motif) on the envelope.

Assemble:

1. Transfer the lettering to the small strip of card stock. Use the scrapbook marker to write the words. *Option:* Write the words freehand.

2. Place the small strip of white card stock at the top of the purple card. Place the white card stock rectangle just beneath the small strip of lettering. Center them and glue in place using glue stick.

3. Glue the painted piece of watercolor paper with the characters to the center of the white card stock using glue stick.

Decorate:

1. Glue the rick-rack to the edges of the card with tacky glue.

2. Put the two small purple flower brads at the sides of the lettering.

3. Put the large flower brads in the corners of the painted design.

4. With the scrapbook marker draw the dotted lines in between the four sections of the card and around the edges. ❏

Pattern for Card (actual size)

Envelope design

Hoppy Easter

By Marni Adams

INSTRUCTIONS

Prepare Card:

1. Fold watercolor paper in half to create horizontal card 5-1/2" x 4-1/4".

2. Trace the pattern and transfer the design to the front of the card (except for shading on bunny's ears and cheeks). Use a kneaded eraser to erase any mistakes.

Color with Watercolor Pencils:

1. With Spanish Orange, color the backgrounds behind the flowers and eggs (using very light pressure), the center of the flower in the top left corner, the top stripe of the egg on the left, and the chick.

2. With Orange, color the center of the flower in the bottom left corner, the top stripe of the egg on the top, the chick's beak, and the two carrots.

3. With Pink, color the background of the "hoppy" and "easter" blocks (using very light pressure), the tulip on the left, the bottom stripe of the egg on the left, the butterfly, and the nose and tail of the bunny.

4. With True Green, color the background (using very light pressure) the tulip leaves, the center stripe of the egg on the left, the greens of the two carrots, and the bottom stripe of the egg on the right.

5. With True Blue, color the backgrounds behind the lamb, bunny, chick, and butterfly (using very light pressure), the flower on the bottom left corner, the bottom stripe of the egg on the top, and the tulip on the right.

6. With Violet, color the flower in the top left corner, the center of the flower on the right, and the top stripe of the egg on the right.

7. With Black, color the ears of the lamb and the body of the butterfly.

8. Wet colored areas with a brush dampened with water. Allow to dry overnight. TIPS: Every time you put the brush in water, blot it on a paper towel. Rinse thoroughly between colors. Use the #6 brush for larger areas and the #2 brush for smaller areas.

Ink:

1. Using the .01 pen, ink the background circles.

2. Using the .08 pen, ink the border lines.

3. Using the .05 pen, ink the remainder of the design.

Color with Colored Pencils:

1. With Pink, add shading to the bunny's ears and cheeks (using the pattern as a guide) and color 12 background circles.

2. With True Blue, color accents on "hoppy" and 12 background circles.

3. With Violet, color accents on "easter" and 12 background circles.

4. With Spanish Orange, color 12 background circles.

5. With Orange, color 12 background circles.

6. With True Green, color remaining background circles. ❑

Pattern for Card (actual size)

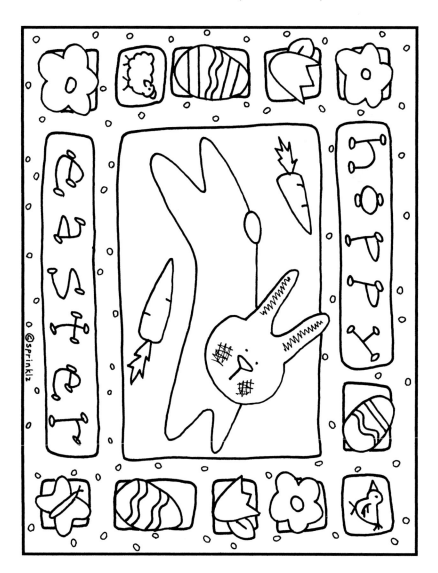

SUPPLIES

Paper:

Dark sage green card stock,
8-1/2" x 11"

Pumpkin orange card stock,
4" x 6", 2-1/2" x 3-1/2", and
2-3/4" x 6"

Yellow dual-sided card stock,
5-1/4" x 2"

Scraps of card stock in fall colors
(for leaves)

1 sheet clear vellum

Tools & Other Supplies:

Punch - Maple leaf

Felt dye ink pads - Meadow,
Rust, Butterscotch, Terra
Cotta

Scissors

Sea sponge, one for each color

Glue stick

Deckle scissors

Tracing paper, transfer paper,
stylus

Vellum tape

Bone folder

INSTRUCTIONS

1. Fold dark sage green card stock in
half to make a card 5-1/2" x 8-
1/2" and crease the fold with a
bone folder.

2. Trim the edges of 2-3/4" x 6"
pumpkin card stock with deckle
scissors.

3. Glue the 4" x 6" pumpkin card
stock to lower right of card, leave
1/4" of green showing at bottom
and right edges.

Autumn Greetings

By Sandra Wilde

Ginger and cinnamon

fill the air

A patchwork of leaves

lay everywhere

Cold, clean mornings

and an indigo dawn

Crystal frost on the

emerald lawn

Golden apple cider and

delicious pumpkin pie

These are the things

I love at Autumntime

4. Using the sponges and the various colors of ink, sponge the 2-3/4" x 6" piece of pumpkin card stock in a random pattern. Glue to upper left of card front, leaving 1/4" of green showing on left side and at top.

5. Fold yellow dual card stock in half lengthwise. Trace pattern and transfer to yellow card stock. Cut on solid lines to form chevrons. Open card. Fold down chevrons on dotted lines. Glue down chevrons. Glue cut piece to upper left of card front.

6. Punch leaves from card stock scraps.

7. Print sentiments on vellum. Cut out with deckle scissors.

8. Using vellum tape, adhere "Ginger and cinnamon" sentiment to the card front, over the pumpkin card stock.

9. Using vellum tape, adhere smaller verse to 2-1/2" x 3-1/2" piece of pumpkin card stock. Adhere inside card.

10. Decorate with punched leaves inside and out. ❑

Place on fold

Pattern for
Chevrons
(actual size)

SUPPLIES

Paper:

White card stock, 7" x 7"

Orange card stock, 4" x 6"

Yellow card stock, 2" x 6"

Green card stock, 1-1/16" x 2-3/8" and 2-1/4" x 3-1/2" (for the envelope)

Black card stock, 1" x 1"

Pink card stock, 1/2" x 1/2"

White copy paper

Tools & Other Supplies:

Black technical pen, .01 *or* computer and printer

Buttons - bat, cat

Round hole punch, 1/4"

4" orange double-faced satin ribbon, 1/8" wide

Tracing paper, transfer paper, stylus

Pencil

Quick dry tacky glue

Ruler

Scissors

Deckle Scissors

Costume Party Invitation

Halloween Card

By Margaret Hanson-Maddox

Decorate Inside:

1. Using a black pen or a computer, print the text of the invitation on copy paper:

   We're inviting you!

   Date:_____

   Time:_____

   Where:_____

   Corny Hosts:_____

   RSVP to:_____

   It's a Costume Party!

INSTRUCTIONS

Make Card:

1. Trace envelope and card patterns on tracing paper. Slip tracing paper between card stock and tracing paper and retrace the pattern pieces with stylus on appropriate card stock colors. Cut out pattern pieces.

2. Using stylus and ruler, score along fold line of white card base.

2. Cut to fit the inside of the card and glue in place. Glue the black cat button above the invitation text.

Decorate Outside:

1. Glue orange and yellow card stock pieces in place, using photo as a guide for placement.

2. Glue eyes in place.

3. Using hole punch, punch two black pupils and glue on eyes. Cut a black triangle nose and glue on face.

4. Using the hole punch, punch two pink cheek circles and glue on face.

5. Using a black pen or computer, print "It's corny, But it's true..." on copy paper. Cut out to measure 7/8" x 2-1/8". Glue on green card stock. Glue mounted words on yellow area of card front.

6. Tie a bow with orange ribbon. Glue to upper right corner of message box.

7. Using the black pen, add eyebrows, eyelashes, and mouth.

8. Glue black bat button on white area of face.

Decorate Envelope:

1. Using deckle scissors, cut the remaining piece of green card stock to create a triangular shape. Glue to lower left corner of envelope.

2. Glue orange and yellow card stock on white card stock to form candy corn.

3. Using hole punch, punch out two white eyes and glue on face. Using the black pen, add eyebrows, eyelashes, pupils, nose, and mouth. ❏

Cut 1 - Orange

Patterns for Card (actual size)

Cut 1 - White

Cut 1 - Orange

Cut 1 - Yellow

Cut 2 - White (Eyes)

Cut 1 - Yellow

Cut 1 - White (Card Base)

Fold line

SUPPLIES

Paper:

140 lb. soft press watercolor
   paper, 5-1/2" x 8-1/2"

Watercolor Pencils:

Black

Crimson Red

Grass Green

Orange

Sunburst Yellow

Violet

Tools & Other Supplies:

Technical pens with black ink,
   .05, .08

Artist brushes - #2 round, #6
   round

Kneaded eraser

Pencil and sharpener

Paper towels

Water container

Tracing paper,
   graphite transfer
   paper, stylus

Scary-Boo
Halloween Card

By Marni Adams

INSTRUCTIONS

Prepare the Card:

1. Fold watercolor paper to create a horizontal card 5-1/2" x 4-1/4".

2. Trace pattern and transfer design to front of card. Use a kneaded eraser to erase
   any mistakes.

Refer to project photo:

Pattern for Card (actual size)

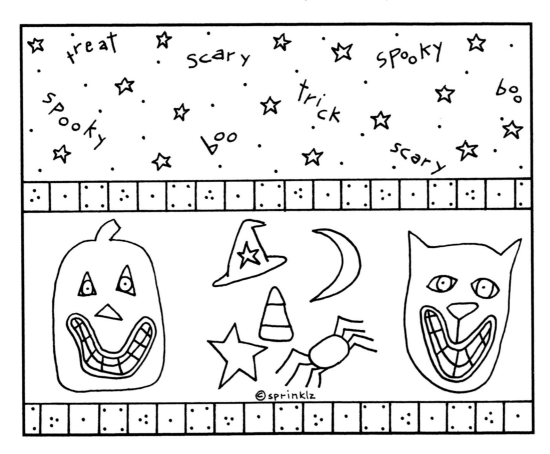

Color:

1. With Sunburst Yellow, color the background stars, the pumpkin's eyes, the star on the hat, the moon, the middle section of the candy corn, the large star, and the cat's eyes.

2. With Orange, color the background of the upper section (using very light pressure), the border squares with four dots, the pumpkin, the bottom section of the candy corn, and the cat's nose.

3. With Crimson Red, color the pumpkin's lips and the cat's lips.

4. With Grass Green, color the border squares with three dots.

5. With Violet, color the border squares with one dot and the background of the lower section (using very light pressure).

6. With Black, color the pumpkin's nose, the hat, the spider, and the cat.

7. Wet the colored areas using a brush dampened with water. Allow to dry overnight. TIPS: Every time you put the brush in water, blot it on a paper towel. Rinse thoroughly between colors. Use the #6 brush for larger areas and the #2 brush for smaller areas.

Ink:

1. Using the .08 pen, ink the border lines and the dots.

2. Using the .05 pen, ink the remainder of the design. ❏

Santa & Stars

Christmas Card

By Karen Embry

Pattern for Card (actual size)

Pattern for Envelope (actual size)

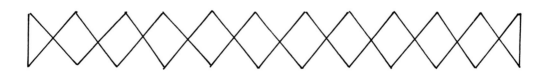

INSTRUCTIONS

Paint:

1. Transfer the design to card and envelope.

2. Paint the diamond shapes and the mouth with Engine Red.

3. Paint the nose and cheeks with Baby Pink. Float the lower edges of the nose and cheeks with Engine Red. Float the top edges of the nose and cheeks with Wicker White.

4. Paint the face with Wicker White + touches of Pumpkin Orange + Baby Pink (a light skin tone).

5. Dot the eyes with Licorice.

6. Paint the beard, band of hat, and pom pom with Wicker White.

7. Outline the pom pom, band, and beard and add swirls on beard with Silver Sterling glitter paint.

Assemble:

1. Glue the ribbon on the edge of the card and on either side of the painted design on the envelope.

2. Punch tiny holes for the brads and attach the silver star brads to the card. ❑

SUPPLIES

Paper:

140 lb. soft press watercolor
paper, 5-1/2" x 8-1/2"

Watercolor Pencils:

Black

Cool Grey 50%

Copenhagen

Crimson Red

Dark Brown

Dark Green

Goldenrod

Indigo Blue

Light Peach

Ultramarine

Colored Pencils:

Crimson Red

Dark Green

**Tools & Other
Supplies:**

Technical pens with
black ink, .05, .08

Artist brushes - #2
round, #6 round

Kneaded eraser

Pencil and sharpener

Paper towels

Water container

Tracing paper, transfer
paper, stylus

Very Merry
Christmas Card

By Marni Adams

INSTRUCTIONS

Prepare Card:

1. Fold watercolor paper in half to create horizontal card 5-1/2" x 4-1/4".
2. Trace the pattern and transfer the design to the front of the card (except the shading on snowman's cheeks, reindeer's cheeks, and Santa's cheeks). Use a kneaded eraser to erase any mistakes.

Color with Watercolor Pencils:

1. With Goldenrod, color the snowman's nose, the star on the snowman's scarf, the large star, the candle flame, the three stars over the trees, and the star on Santa's belt.
2. With Light Peach, color Santa's face and hands.

122

Pattern for Card (actual size)

3. With Crimson Red, color alternating stripes on the snowman's stockings, the background hearts, the large heart, the house, half the small sections in the striped border, the stripes on the candy canes, Rudolph's nose, Santa's hat, alternating sections in Santa's hat cuff, Santa's nose, Santa's suit, and alternating stripes on Santa's stockings.

4. With Copenhagen, color the background behind the snowman.

5. With Ultramarine, color the background behind Santa and Rudolph.

6. With Indigo Blue, color the background behind the house and the trees and the candle.

7. With Dark Green, color the snowman's scarf, the remaining stripes on the snowman's stockings, the three trees, the remaining small sections in the striped border, the background behind the candy canes, the remaining sections in Santa's hat cuff, and the remaining stripes on Santa's stockings.

8. With Cool Grey, color the large sections in the striped border and the pom pom on Santa's hat.

9. With Dark Brown, color the snowman's buttons, the background behind the large heart, star, and candle, the house roof, the background behind "very merry," and Rudolph.

10. With Black, color the snowman's eyes, the chimney, the windows and door of the house, and Santa's belt.

11. Wet the colored areas using a brush dampened with water. Allow to dry overnight. TIPS: Every time you put the brush in water, blot it on a paper towel. Rinse thoroughly between colors. Use the #6 brush for larger areas and the #2 brush for smaller areas.

Ink:

1. Using the .08 pen, ink the border lines.
2. Using the .05 pen, ink the remainder of the design.

Color with Colored Pencils:

1. With Dark Green, color "very."
2. With Crimson Red, color "merry," and add shading to cheeks on snowman, Rudolph, and Santa, using the pattern as a guide. ❑

SUPPLIES

Paper:

140 lb. soft press watercolor paper, 11" x 8-1/2"

Watercolor Pencils:

Black

Carmine Red

Cool Grey (50%)

Copenhagen

Cream

Crimson Red

Dark Brown

Dark Green

Dark Umber

French Grey (20%)

Goldenrod

Grass Green

Indigo Blue

Light Peach

Olive Green

Sienna Brown

Spanish Orange

Colored Pencils:

Carmine Red

Crimson Red

Tools & Other Supplies:

Technical pens with black ink, .01, .05, .08

Artist brushes - #2 round, #6 round

Kneaded eraser

Pencil and sharpener

Ruler

Paper towels

Water container

Tracing paper, graphite transfer paper, stylus

Patterns are found on page 126.

Country Quartet
Christmas Card

By Marni Adams

INSTRUCTIONS

Prepare:

1. Fold watercolor paper in half to create a vertical card 5-1/2" x 8-1/2".

2. Trace pattern with tracing paper. Using graphite paper, transfer design to front of card (except for shading lines on reindeer's ears). Use a kneaded eraser to erase any mistakes.

Color with Watercolor Pencils:

1. With Cream, color the snowman.

2. With French Grey, color Santa's beard and the angel's face.

3. With Cool Grey, color the angel's collar.

4. With Light Peach, color Santa's face.

5. With Spanish Orange, color two of the stars on Santa's hat and the stars on the snowman's scarf.

6. With Goldenrod, color the remaining two stars on Santa's hat and the snowman's nose.

7. With Carmine Red, color Santa's nose and the hearts on the snowman's scarf.

8. With Crimson Red, color Santa's hat, the berries on the angel's collar, the hearts on the angel's dress, the berries around the reindeer's neck, and the reindeer's nose.

9. With Grass Green, color the holly leaves on the angel's collar, the middle row of trees, and the holly leaves around the reindeer's neck.

10. With Olive Green, color the top row of trees and the snowman's scarf.

11. With Dark Green, color the trim and pom pom on Santa's hat and the bottom row of trees.

12. With Copenhagen, color the background behind the angel and the background behind the reindeer.

13. With Indigo Blue, color the background behind Santa, the angel's dress, and the background behind the snowman.

14. With Sienna Brown, color the angel's wings, the trunks of the middle row of trees, the reindeer's antlers, and the background behind the bottom row of trees.

15. With Dark Brown, color the background behind the top row of trees, the reindeer, and the trunks of the bottom row of trees.

16. With Dark Umber, color the trunks of the top row of trees and the background behind the middle row of trees.

17. With Black, color Santa's eyes, the angel's eyes, the reindeer's eyes, and the snowman's eyes, mouth, and buttons.

18. Wet the colored areas, using a brush dampened with water. Allow to dry overnight. TIPS: Every time you put the brush in water, blot it on a paper towel. Rinse thoroughly between colors. Use the #6 brush for larger areas and the #2 brush for smaller areas.

Ink:

1. Using the .08 pen, ink the border lines and the dots.

2. Using the .01 pen, ink the cheeks and the background patterns behind the three rows of trees.

3. Using the .05 pen, ink the remainder of the design.

Color with Colored Pencils:

1. With Carmine Red, color the angel's cheeks, the shading on the reindeer's ears (see the pattern), the reindeer's cheeks, and the stripes behind the middle row of trees.

2. With Crimson Red, color Santa's cheeks, the angel's nose, the snowman's cheeks, and the pattern lines behind the top and bottom rows of trees. ❏

Pattern for
Country
Quartet

*Instructions begin
on page 125.*

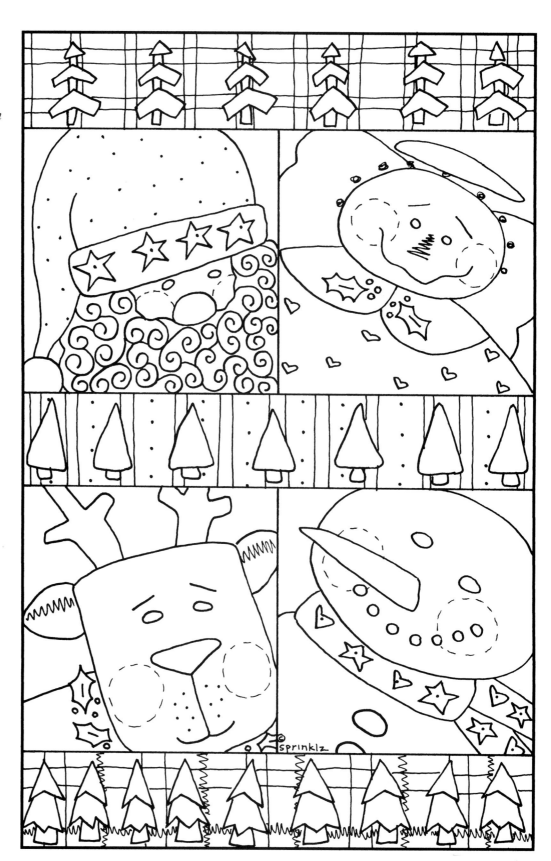

Metric Conversion Chart

Inches to Millimeters and Centimeters

Inches	MM	CM	Inches	MM	CM
1/8	3	.3	2	51	5.1
1/4	6	.6	3	76	7.6
3/8	10	1.0	4	102	10.2
1/2	13	1.3	5	127	12.7
5/8	16	1.6	6	152	15.2
3/4	19	1.9	7	178	17.8
7/8	22	2.2	8	203	20.3
1	25	2.5	9	229	22.9
1-1/4	32	3.2	10	254	25.4
1-1/2	38	3.8	11	279	27.9
1-3/4	44	4.4	12	305	30.5

Yards to Meters

Yards	Meters
1/8	.11
1/4	.23
3/8	.34
1/2	.46
5/8	.57
3/4	.69
7/8	.80
1	.91
2	1.83
3	2.74
4	3.66
5	4.57
6	5.49
7	6.40
8	7.32
9	8.23
10	9.14

Index

Continued on next page

Index (continued)